FORCE
OF
PERSUASION

FORCE OF PERSUASION

Dynamic Techniques for Influencing People

FORREST H. PATTON

PRENTICE HALL PRESS

New York London Toronto Sydney Tokyo

Published by Prentice Hall Press
A Division of Simon & Schuster, Inc.
Gulf+Western Building
One Gulf+Western Plaza
New York, New York 10023

PRENTICE HALL PRESS is a trademark of Simon & Schuster, Inc.

Library of Congress Cataloging-in-Publication Data

Patton, Forrest H.
    Force of persuasion.

    Includes index.
    1. Persuasion (Psychology)   2. Interpersonal communication.   I. Title.
BF637.P4P34   1986   153.8′52   86-9477
ISBN 0-13-325127-6

Designed by Stanley S. Drate/Folio Graphics Co. Inc.
Manufactured in the United States of America

10   9   8   7   6   5   4   3   2

CONTENTS

In my years of selling I've always been fascinated by what *really* influences people. The sequence of getting attention, interest, desire, and action isn't enough. We all have very real, private feelings that are often masked by smiles, handshakes, and polite friendliness. When we try to influence another person both parties will usually have an undercurrent of positive or negative feelings. These hidden feelings frequently determine the success or failure of our persuasion effort.

I wanted to pin those feelings down. I wanted to find out what caused them and what one could do to influence those feelings positively—both in oneself and in the other person. This book is a result of that study. It identifies the emotional swings and cravings of people and tells how to deal with these in the process of negotiation and persuasion.

The most exciting part of formulating this method of influencing others has been the new revelations in neurophysiological research and the link to positive thinking. Neuroscientists now show us that positive thinking is more than a nice idea. Positive thoughts and negative thoughts physically trigger certain neurotransmitters and electrochemical action in our brains that form networks, or Mind Sets. These very physical Mind Sets affect all areas of our being and our attitudes. They directly affect the way we influence others. Best of all, we can choose the kind of Mind Sets that we want.

These chapters show the precise method of programming these Mind Sets to higher selling, influencing, and achieving. We are in charge. We are truly the captains of our lives. This book is the navigation chart. In producing it I owe a debt of gratitude to numerous neuroscientists, psychologists, and parapsychologists for their invaluable input and writings.

1

Your Aura of Influence

*K*aren Carter sat down, gingerly, on the red leather chair outside the CEO's office. A new position at the company had opened and she wanted it very much. The new responsibility would be quite a step up. She knew she was qualified, but would it be given to a woman?

Anxiety was building, and she hated the feeling. Should she have worn the jacket or the blazer with the tailored skirt? The white blouse or the paisley blouse? Would she do the right things, say the right things to influence Mr. Arnold?

Inside, Steve Jackson was trying to sell Mr. Arnold on a new microfilm service. Steve had a warm manner and made a fair enough presentation. He knew his product. The benefits made sense. But something about Steve bothered Dave Arnold. An uneasy intuitive feeling influenced him to put the decision off. As he pushed his chair back from the desk, he was glad Steve took the cue that it was time to leave.

Just after Steve left, a panicky thought raced through Dave Arnold's mind. Somehow, sometime today, he had to put together the key points he would make to the board of directors tomorrow morning. Would they buy his idea of two new distribution centers? How could he persuade Martin and Ed, who nitpicked every new idea? Facing his own dilemma, he could not give Steve Jackson or Karen Carter his full attention.

Whether you are in Karen Carter's situation, Steve Jackson's, or Dave Arnold's, persuading another person doesn't have to be a hit-or-miss affair. No longer must we be so careful that our "masks" are on just right to cover inner anxiety, self-doubt, or plain shyness. New brain patterns of boldness, confidence, and commitment can be learned and practiced to offset such insecurities.

Neuroscientists have made exciting new breakthroughs concerning how we develop patterns of thought and how these patterns affect the way we act, and thus, how we influence the actions of others. Actual vibrations of energy coming from a person can now be photographed. In fact, a person's emotional attitude determines the varied colors registered in the photographs. The "vibes" you feel from another person are very real, indeed.

We all know that confident thinking, feeling, and acting affects the way we influence others. Now neuropsychologists and neurophysiologists have opened the doors that link such thinking to certain electrochemical patterns of thought. With a system of mental programming, we can arrange the neuron patterns that we want, which, in turn, form the *Mind Sets* of positive influence with others.

That does not mean that every persuasion attempt will have the positive result we want. There will be times of stress, such as the examples above. But by forming these Mind Sets, the "batting average" of positive influence on ourselves and others will increase dramatically.

Let's analyze this for a moment. Our thoughts are not stored like a file system or linearly like a computer, but spread in a shimmering flash through a network of hairlike dendrites making interacting connections between the billions of neuron cells. These networks of connections form the Mind Sets that are the result of our emotional experiences and type of thinking. It is these Mind Sets that determine the way we habitually come across to others and what we attract in life.

The chapters in this book spell out precisely how to form these Mind Sets. By forming the Mind Sets that we choose, we will be mastering the forces of persuasion. We will influence the kind of "chemistry" with others that we want to take place. Our private thoughts are not totally private. They affect our manner, our appearance, the way we express ourselves. They influence the feelings that are picked up by others intuitively. Our private self-talk is a very real force that can either repel or attract another. Our Mind Sets determine our self-confidence and persuasive ability to achieve the life-style we want. The beauty is that we can both select and formulate the Mind Sets we wish.

Studies and experiments back up what we have long sensed: By changing our thought patterns or Mind Sets, we can change our habits, our health, and our state of happiness. We can and do attract what we program into our minds. We are virtual sending and receiving stations of thought forces. William James once said that the greatest discovery of the century was not in physical science but in the power of the subconscious mind.

Physicist David Bohm concludes that all is pure vibration, or forces of frequency, and our perception is a reaction to these frequency vibrations. Robert M. Anderson, writing for the *Journal of Transpersonal Psychology*, holds that reality, as we know it, is constructed on the basis of holographic vibration principles.

We are a kind of transmitter and receiver with our private thoughts emitting vibrations like radio transmissions. By using the methods and practices on the following pages, you will influence others in a most positive and productive way.

We're all selling and persuading. An artist, an architect, or a CPA sells an idea to a prospective client. A dentist sells a patient on a full-mouth restoration. The president sells his budget program on TV. Parents sell children on getting good grades. Children sell parents on places to take them or food to buy. A teacher sells interest in a subject to the pupils. A boss sells employees on company goals. Employees sell bosses on better working conditions. A wife sells her husband on a certain investment she wants to make. The husband sells the wife on a certain investment *he* wants to make.

And 8,383,000 salespeople keep the economy spinning by selling more and more services and products. The outcome of this selling is very dependent on the sellers' quality of thinking . . . the kind of Mind Sets they have chosen.

THE FOUR FORCES OF INFLUENCE

Moment to moment, we are pouring out a steady stream of influencing forces that either benefit us or hinder us. These four forces not only influence how others react to us, but determine our achievements or lack of achievements in life. These forces influence the state of our health and our degree of zest.

This entire book is a how-to manual in forming intense, positive Mind Sets. You will see how the four forces overlap and mesh with one another. You will experience the immediate results of these new, positive Mind Sets as they take hold in each of the four areas of influence.

The Force of Senses

Mind Sets can be formed on influencing others positively through the five senses. This includes how we dress and our confident manner in the way we walk and speak. It is our warmth, poise, and spontaneity in the way we present ourselves.

If our private self-talk is confident, optimistic, and caring, we will project this with a sparkle in the eye, good posture, a genuine smile, and empathy for the other person. It will be reflected in our enthusiasm and manner—even in the clothes we choose to wear. It will show in our timing, our ability to communicate benefits, and get positive commitment from others. It will come across in our ability to listen with concern.

The Force of Tactics

We influence others through various tactics. Mind Sets of techniques are spelled out in many of the following chapters, such as "Concentration and Perception," "Your Personality Style," "Your New Super Memory," "Motivating Others," "Negotiating Strategy," and "Negotiating Tactics."

We are using the positive force of tactics when we observe and learn about the personal interests of others. Tactics includes the ability to ask the right questions and then really listen to the answers. Tactics is getting across that we are authorities, or using short anecdotes to show that others use our services or products. It is employing the power of giving something, knowing that human nature wants to reciprocate. It is appealing to consistency of behavior by winning minor points to condition one for major concessions. Together with the force of senses, it is combining friendliness with being as attractive as possible. It is also using "negative sell" or giving the impression that something is hard to get, or expensive, and therefore exceptional or only for "special" people. The force of tactics includes all the subtleties of first finding and then appealing to the hungry wants of the ego. Taking advantage of intuitive feedback certainly must be included as a tactic.

The Force of Character

These are the intuitive "vibes" people pick up about us. If we have the right self-talk, or Mind Sets, people pick up depth of character, honesty, dependability, sincerity, intelligence, how much we care about them, and the values that we have. This aura of influence is a very powerful force.

How one is perceived intuitively has much to do with that person's influence with another. Many important decisions are based on this gut feeling. A nationwide employment agency, studying hiring decisions, found that the average yes-or-no decision time was five minutes! The decision-maker had mentally decided very early in the interview, even though much more time was spent going through formalities. Most likely, the majority of the decisions were a blend of both the senses and the intuitive feedback of character.

In selling, the most critical time is the first three minutes. That's when the strongest physical and intuitive judgments about a person are being made. A constant undercurrent of wrong thinking is not hidden. The smile and glad hand will not cover it up. Oh, it sometimes works for a while when someone wants to believe what he hears and temporarily shuts out the intuitive messages. Dislike, contempt, resentment, jealousy, connivance, manipulation, cheating, and lying are not hidden. The vibrations are there to be picked up by another. They take their toll in negative influence.

The Force of Expectancy

One of the most powerful forces of persuasion is the expectancy that it will happen. It includes ego drive, faith, positive thinking, confidence, and persistence. Those who formulate and harness this Mind Set have harnessed an awesome activator.

Others frequently respond to this force automatically. A warm, assumptive attitude seems to draw people to acts of commitment. It combines with the "force of senses" to influence the right choice of words, manner, and body language.

There is another part to the force of expectancy. It is the area of influence that brings about the things or conditions desired. This expectancy of one's strong emotional desires is, perhaps, projected or transmitted much like the pulsations of a radio transmitter.

At this moment the vibrations from many radio transmitters are surrounding your body with thirty to sixty songs and voices. But you don't hear them. If your interest were soft rock, however, you might tune to that station. In much the same way, conditions and people are "drawn" and "tuned in" to our strong commitments, to our expectancy attitude. As you become emotionally intense in your interests and constantly "see" or "feel" the end result, the transmission becomes very powerful. Events and circumstances fall into place. You have employed the force of expectancy.

Let's tie this together. Our consistent thought patterns or Mind Sets determine how we influence people and what we accomplish. Science has provided us with new insights into how these Mind Sets are formed and how they influence our lives.

The exciting thing is that you and I can plan and program the various Mind Sets that we want. We can change, alter, or reinforce our *four forces of influence*. We are in the driver's seat. We can choose the muddy roads of mediocrity or a life of fulfillment and fascinating achievements. This book is the road map on how to accomplish it by programming new neuron patterns in the brain.

The self-influencing system in these chapters is based on the latest advances in neurophysiology. By using this system of forming new Mind Sets you can change tough-to-break habits such as smoking, free yourself from anxiety, get out of boring, unproductive ruts to achieve an efficient, highly productive life-style.

Putting this system to work places a person in the mainstream of charged energy, youthful appearance, a radiant personality, and increased income. For the business person it is a very detailed guide on strategy, negotiating, and "closing the sale." Whatever your path in life, it is the method of programming the forces of persuasion to a new height of achievement.

2

Programming Your Mind

A most awesome thing is taking place as you are reading this sentence. One hundred thousand separate chemical reactions are taking place in your brain every second! Each one of the billions of neurons in your brain is hard at work this moment synthesizing chemicals and proteins that move down to the 10 trillion synapse gaps. The chemical is fired into the gaps between neurons, enabling the electrical charge of thought to pass from one neuron to another. What a fantastic brain interplay is going on when you are selling, persuading, or influencing another.

In *The Brain Book* published by E. P. Dutton, Inc., brain research psychologist Peter Russell explains that each one of your neurons has up to 10 thousand of these connections with other neurons; that if these hairlike dentrites in your brain were strung out they would reach one hundred thousand miles. Most important from the standpoint of programming your mind is the fact that new neuron connections are being made constantly. Just as soon as you have a feeling about something, new connections are being formed among millions of neurons. As you continue to have that feeling or opinion, these connections are reinforced.

Positive Thinking Is Actually a Physiological Mind Set

Reinforced connections form a Mind Set. It is a physical thing that is happening in your brain. It affects the way you sell and influence others. It affects your health, your habits, what you have and what you don't have in life. All of us have known about the benefits of

7

thinking positively. But the idea has always been rather nebulous. Scientific breakthroughs are showing us physiologically what it is, how it affects us, and what it will do for us.

We are truly on the threshold of finding out how to use this powerful tool of thought. We've known the power was there, but most of us have had a healthy skepticism. Certainly there are plenty of references in the Bible about the power of thought. Emerson and other philosophers have spelled it out. But there have also been the charlatans, the proponents of how to instantly change your life.

It doesn't change instantly; I found that out. Probably like you, I always knew these powerful forces were there. Yet, I would apply them only sometimes. It was as if part of me believed in them and the other part didn't. The idea of using meditation sounded interesting. When I first tried it I practiced for twenty minutes a day for three days and then lost interest. I remember going to one of those positive thinking rallies and getting all charged up, but the next day things were pretty much back to normal. How come? Did it work for others and not for me? Is the positive thinking thing just one big hype?

I found some answers, most of them through trial and error. Yes, positive thinking does work. Yes, there is some hype out there. In this chapter I will separate the hype from the real. There are some precise reasons why it doesn't seem to work all of the time. The why and the how are very important to anyone with a practical bent and, certainly, the why and how are vitally important to those of us who persuade and sell.

Mind Programming Is the Road to High Achievement

Those recent discoveries of how thoughts form a Mind Set are critical to changing your own life. They point the way to a realistic new process of influencing greatness into your own sphere of living. They show the way to high achievement whether it's in selling, any other profession, or finding one's way out of a myriad of problems. Forming your new Mind Set is the way to meaningful relationships, zest, and good health. The method of changing the things you want changed is here. We owe a debt of gratitude to the great philosophers, the visionaries, and the scientists who have moved us to this point.

In this chapter we're going to walk through, step by step, the method of programming patterns in your brain. By repeating certain affirmations each day you will reinforce those patterns until they become a Mind Set. This will affect your achievements and the way you influence others.

You will experience the frequently dramatic changes in your own attitude and how these, in turn, change the reaction of others toward you. These are very real forces in the complex brain patterns of the Mind Set. These new patterns you program will enhance your appearance, youthfulness, reactive time, concentration, memory, and self-motivation to action. You will experience a wonderful release in being your own person, rather than daily reacting to existing conditions and pressures imposed by other people. In making sales calls, this kind of thinking is the way to productivity of the highest sort.

How a Positive Affirmation Works . . . and Doesn't Work

Let's say you want to program into your life a very high degree of self-confidence. Daily, you could use the affirmation, "I am bold. I am very self-confident." If you say that silently, there will be many connections made between various neurons in your brain. In fact, a great number of connections were just made as you read it. But if you say it out loud, you now involve an entire additional network of connections. Your very inflections on the words affect the connections. Also, hearing yourself may well trigger some emotional feelings about being bold. Strong emotional feelings produce a much wider network in the brain. If the affirmation is something you *emotionally* want, then the connections are very much increased.

Now, let's suppose that as a child you were very shy. That network of new connections would have to compete with a well-reinforced Mind Set of past experiences. Those experiences would have been strongly lodged in the brain since childhood. To overcome this you would have to say the affirmation and also *visualize* the affirmation of boldness and confidence. An example would be imagining yourself smoothly introducing a number of people to one another, or confidently making a winning presentation to two steely-eyed buyers. As far as the brain is concerned, you would now be adding *experience*. Your brain would go through the experience and make the connections as though the event were actually taking place.

Let's see what can go wrong with that affirmation of boldness and confidence. Suppose you made the affirmation this morning. Also, suppose it was the first time you did any mind programming. Now you are out there making a call on a prospect and you're sitting across the desk from the president of the company. As you reach over to point out something on the price list, a file in your lap falls and sends papers all over the floor. Flustered, you gather them up. It was just a small accident, but it bothers you. You feel embarrassed as you get back to discussing prices.

"That price is too high," the president says as he looks right at you. You feel your eyes go down as you try to handle the objection, but you realize your answer wasn't confidently stated. Later, in the car, you feel a bit disgusted with yourself. You didn't perform very confidently. Faith in those positive affirmations certainly hasn't been enhanced.

What went wrong? Nothing, really. You can't expect a one-time set of new connections to change the strong, reinforced connections of years. Let's say you've had inadequate feelings before. So, you already had a Mind Set of very strong interneuron connections that you are sometimes shy. The experience you just went through reinforced it with more connections. Where were the bold, self-confident connections when you needed them? They simply weren't strong enough yet. The old Mind Set took over; the new Mind Set was not established. That simple example of not getting immediate results is one of the reasons people doubt the effectiveness of affirmations.

For that affirmation to form a new Mind Set you would, first, have to emotionally want it, not just logically think that you ought to have it. Next, you would have to make that affirmation every day—or nearly every day for thirty to sixty days. This would help you reinforce the *belief* that you were getting more confident every day. Finally, you might say the affirmation in different ways to keep it emotionally interesting.

That is the price. The affirmations do work, but you must work at them constantly—and in an interesting, *feeling* manner. Just reciting a group of affirmations daily is helpful, but not nearly as meaningful as getting feeling and emotion and visualization into it. That's why you have to really want it. Otherwise, it won't be emotionally important to you.

This is the reason so many good intentions don't work. It explains why we continue habits we supposedly want to change.

Logically, we shouldn't smoke or overeat. Logically, we should make more new sales calls, with good follow-up letters and calls. Logically, we should be well organized and manage ourselves and our time correctly. But we're emotional. Probably 90 percent of all our thinking is emotional. To change conditions we have to want them emotionally and then program them into the brain as *experiences* that are already happening. With continuous repetition, the doubts about whether the programming will succeed fade, the neuron connections are reinforced, and the outward condition takes place.

Program the Exact Mind Set You Want

What fantastic potential each one of us has. Yet, how few know it or know what to do about it. If we want to condition our bodies, we know what to do, we work at it daily. But few people know how to condition a new Mind Set, and attract what they want in life.

What about those very successful men and women who never bought self-help books on positive thinking. I know some of them never practiced any meditation whatsoever, and they seem to have done quite well. What about their Mind Sets?

Just talk to any of them. They are practicing mind conditioning constantly. They do control their thinking. They get very restless around negative, nitpicking, fearful, self-doubting losers. Their thoughts are well directed to large issues, specific goals, and successful conclusions. They are reinforcing their Mind Sets daily. A great many highly successful people do, of course, regularly practice meditation, and daily read something to reinforce their positive attitude.

Let's start right now to lock in the specific conditions in your life that you really want. We're going into the "how" in a moment. A word of warning: There will be a period in about three or four days or maybe a week or two when the novelty wears off and you begin to skip days, then a few weeks, and finally forget about it. I've been there too. So, I'm going to inject a few things that I hope will hold you in there until the results start happening. Some of the things you program may take awhile. But wouldn't it take awhile to program in how to play the piano, or learn to type? Stay with it. If you backslide for a while just get back on course. Form this simple habit that can do so much for you. Truly, you are in for a beautiful treat!

What you program becomes part of you. You and the condition or object become one. A sort of fusion takes place. What I am going to do is guide you in a very intense way of forming millions or billions of new connections; trace patterns in your brain that will, in turn, influence the conditions that you want in your life. You must be emotionally committed to the conditions. Commitment changes lives. Commitment is the big influencer.

Shortly, you will go through the process of mental commitment to the things or conditions you want. You will program a Mind Set of exactly what you want in life. It must be what *you* really want, not what someone else wants, and not what someone else wants you to want.

You are now going to make contact with your subconscious mind through meditation. There is nothing mysterious or mystic about this. In fact, at first you may experience nothing more than being a bit more relaxed. Learning to go into deep, relaxed meditation is the key to influencing your own Mind Set of changed conditions or habits, wonderful relationships, excellent health, youthful, vibrant appearance, and high achievement in selling or any other career.

A Trip to Alpha 10

Our subconscious "comfort zone" is what we believe about ourselves. It is where the subconscious mind feels we belong. It is our present Mind Set that puts a cap on our accomplishments and income. It is responsible for our self-doubts.

When we try to change things to get out of this comfort zone the mind churns up fears and reasons why it won't work. To change the limits of our comfort zone, we must *reprogram* the subconscious mind. This is best done at the alpha level of thought.

Most of our waking activity is spent in the beta zone of brain waves, or about twenty cycles per second. When we are in a relaxed, meditative state, though, our brain waves are functioning at eight to thirteen cycles per second. For programming our mind and relieving stress, our target will be in the neighborhood of Alpha 10.

We're an impatient society. We want instant results. However, the process of changing a condition by mind programming is usually gradual. The exception is that you'll experience immediate relief from stress.

There's another hurdle . . . priority. As great as meditation is, we tend to let other things get in the way. If you get up at seven to go to work, you're probably rushing to get dressed or get the kids off to school. And if you're driving to work, you find that you just don't have time to pull off somewhere and meditate.

Then there's finding the place. At work, if you go to the rest room for fifteen minutes, people may wonder if you have a problem. In the evening finding just ten minutes anywhere without the phone or some other interruption may be difficult. Yet, it is essential that you are alone without a nagging feeling that someone will walk in. It's just normal to be a little self-conscious about sitting there looking weird with your eyes closed.

I point all this out because you're going to run into one or more of these problems. Somehow, each day, in your own hectic pattern, you must find a block of time for yourself. This is so important that the first affirmations in Deep Alpha will be to develop self-discipline. It's not as dull as it may sound. The affirmation would go something like this: "I am my own person. I have the self-discipline to accomplish exactly what I want. I have the discipline to spend at least ten minutes a day in concentrated meditation on my objectives." We want to set up those neuron connections so you will do this each day, week in and week out. You are setting up your first programmed habit. If, after two weeks, you are doing the mind programming each day, you can drop this affirmation if you wish.

The second thing to program may seem strange at first. We want to get rid of toxic thinking. It holds us back. We all indulge in some of this, and certain amounts of toxic thought will continue to seep through. But we can knock out so much of it by a single daily practice. First, read the chapter "Toxic Thinking." I use the term *toxic thinking* instead of negative thinking because it is literally toxic to your body. In that chapter you will see just how it destroys health, appearance, happiness, and opportunities in life. You will immediately handle toxic thinking with a very positive affirmation. It may seem unusual, but it works. Use these words or your own: "I will raise the self-esteem of at least one person today."

Raising Another's Self-Esteem Destroys Toxic Thinking

This is powerful programming! You'll see the almost magical influence it has on you and on others. People don't get enough "lifts" in life. There is the deep longing for approval, for attention. The crying need to think well of one's self is in every one of us. The greatest gift you can possibly give others today is the gift of raising their self-esteem, making them feel better about themselves. This can be a compliment about people's work, their smiles, the way they did something, how smart they were in some decision, their particular ability . . . anything, but it must be sincere.

After this kind of programming in your brain the intraneuron connections are set up so that you *automatically* become more perceptive and look for the good in others. You become more charismatic. It affects your own attitude, and definitely reduces toxic thinking. It takes you out of yourself, makes you more concerned, observant, empathetic, and understanding of others. And oh what a joy you are to be around. The great persuaders have this quality.

I watched Bud Hadfield, president of the worldwide Kwik-Kopy Printing Corporation, as he showed me through his plant employing several hundred people. There was a compliment here, approval there, a pat on the shoulder. The people would beam as he approached. What a great employee/employer attitude. But it has to be real—100 percent honest.

Some of those compliments are hard to let out at first. You wonder, what will people think if you compliment them. Will they think I'm trying to butter them up? Will I be misunderstood? Will I sound gooey, or phony? No, not one bit, if you really mean it. You'll be very pleasantly remembered.

You will not only be raising that person's self-esteem, you'll be raising your own. Nothing but good will come from this daily practice. Remember, you're looking for just *one* person each day. However, you don't have to limit it to one. And you probably won't as you see what it does for yourself and for others. You don't have to plan it. Just be spontaneous with whoever you meet during the course of a day. It lifts the other person, and it lifts you. After a few weeks, when it becomes a daily habit, you can drop it as an affirmation if you wish.

Programming in Deep Alpha

Let's go into Deep Alpha. Find a comfortable chair. Do not lie down. You want to get in the habit of being able to quickly go into Deep Alpha anywhere; at your desk, waiting in an outer office, in airports. Although playing certain types of classical music may be helpful, I suggest you not form the habit for the same reasons. It won't always be available to you.

Meditate any way you see fit. There is no one best way. There is no best time, although you may want to do this in the morning to help program the day. You don't need a group. You don't need a special sound or mantra, though many have found this helpful in concentrating.

Tell yourself that you are going into deep relaxation, into Deep Alpha, that you are going to program your mind, your body, and your life. Pick whatever words you wish or method you wish. There are times I find it helpful to say the thoughts out loud. It's a matter of choice. You may wish to vary that since, at times, you will be going into Deep Alpha when you're in public, perhaps on an airplane or waiting in a lobby. Read through the following several times and then put it in your own words, counting your way from nineteen to ten: "I am now going into Deep Alpha. I am going into deep meditation. I am going to program my mind, my body, and my life. I am very relaxed . . . very relaxed. All the tension is going out of my face, my neck, my shoulders, my back . . . all out of my arms . . . and right out of my fingertips. My body is completely relaxed. All the tension is leaving my body now . . . all the tension is leaving my legs . . . going right out of my toes. I am very relaxed.

"I am going down into Deep Alpha. . . . I will program into my mind self-discipline and raising the self-esteem of other people I meet and know. I'm going down now to Alpha 10. Nineteen . . . deeper, eighteen . . . all the tension is leaving my fingertips. All the tension is going right out my toes. Seventeen . . . I am completely relaxed . . . very relaxed. Sixteen, deeper. Fifteen, deeper . . . deeper . . . deeper. Fourteen . . . I am now getting into Deep Alpha. Thirteen, let go, let go . . . all the tension is out of my body."

(If any area feels tight, such as the neck, say "All the tension is leaving my face . . . out of my neck . . . and out through my fingertips.")

"I am completely relaxed. Twelve . . . deeper . . . deeper . . . eleven . . . ten. I am now in Deep Alpha."

Stay in this state for a few minutes. Your eyes are closed. Thoughts will come racing in; just try to ignore them. You are trying to get into a nonthinking state. But don't be concerned if thoughts continue to flow. This nonthinking state becomes easier the more you go into Deep Alpha. And I hope you won't be disappointed if all sorts of weird things don't happen. They won't.

At first you may feel nothing more than relaxation. That's excellent. At times you will experience going "deeper," and you will have a serene sense of euphoria. You may occasionally drift into a few minutes of sleep. Nothing is wrong with this. It will be quite refreshing. However, if that happens, and you haven't programmed your mind, go right back into Deep Alpha and into the programming.

"I am now going to program my mind and my life and my body. I am my own person. I have the self-discipline to accomplish exactly what I want. I have the self-discipline to spend at least ten minutes a day in concentrated meditation on my objectives. The most important thing I do each day is this meditation. I am getting better and better at it each day. I accept this. It is now programmed."

(In all programming try to add some visual. In this case, see yourself sitting as you are, meditating.)

"Today I will help raise the self-esteem of at least one person. I will find something about that person to comment on. I will be open and spontaneous with this comment. Each day I am becoming more perceptive and more interested in the uniqueness and great qualities in others. I accept this. It is now programmed."

Now, as you wish, program in two or three other things. For example, "Today, I have great stamina and energy." Or, "Today, I make excellent presentations. . . . I close easily and very effectively." Or, "I am earning $———a year." Do not use any other affirmations if you are programming the habits of nonsmoking, losing weight, and cutting down on alcohol. See the chapter "Getting Rid of Stupid Habits" for these. After every affirmation end with, "I accept this; it is now programmed."

Before getting out of the meditation I find the following very powerful. You may wish to change it or put it in your own words.

"I am one with all love, all beauty . . . music . . . flowers . . . trees . . . clouds . . . the body. That love is flowing through me, keeping me in great health. I feel this flowing through me and out to others all day today. I accept this. It is now programmed.

"I am one with all energy. It is coming in from all directions. It is flowing through my body completely . . . giving me great zest, enthusiasm, and stamina all day today. I accept this. It is now programmed.

"I am one with all intelligence. I am open to the great sea of intuitive ideas and directions. I take action today on these ideas and directions. I accept this. It is now programmed.

"I am now refreshed and going back up to Beta . . . ten, eleven, twelve, thirteen, fourteen, fifteen, sixteen, seventeen, eighteen, nineteen, twenty."

Your eyes are open. You may feel calm. You may feel like one big smile. You may jump up, ready to do the things you've planned. The biggest hump is the first few weeks, getting in the habit. When you backslide, as you may, don't feel guilty or accept a haphazard method of meditating. Get right back with it on a daily basis.

One comment before going further. Meditation is simply a tool to fashion your life the way you want it to be. You don't want to become obsessed with the tool. We're meant to be active. Meditation is not a way to get things done without being active. Sitting and meditating or contemplating for hours on end takes that tool out of perspective.

After a meditative period things usually seem to go on as before. You may get in your car, have hate thoughts toward someone, get irritated with another driver, feel anxious about a piece of business, but gradual changes are very definitely taking place in your thinking and in the way you are being drawn to the circumstances you want in life. Millions and millions of new interconnections have taken place physically in your brain to influence the changes. You are growing and changing day by day. It's a little like watching the grass grow. You may not be aware of the changes each day, but they are there. Stay with the program.

This chapter is really the keystone of the book. Mind programming will enhance your negotiating, your memory, your perception, your concentration, and your charisma. It smooths the way through problems, objections, and getting the commitment of others. Best of all, mind programming puts you on a course in life that *you* conditioned and charted.

3

Toxic Thinking

All the techniques of persuasion, all the methods of dressing for success, all those good contacts are worthless if the Mind Set of the brain isn't right.

Undercurrents of hate and resentment and practices of gouging and dishonesty and taking unfair advantage will undermine it all. Such feelings or activity over a period of time will weave a pattern in the brain that will physically interfere with the endocrine glandular balance. This will eventually show up in poor facial tone, possibly ill health, uneasiness, anxiety, unsatisfying materialism, and pitiful, frantic chasing of satisfactions that never seem to please.

There is still another kind of thinking that is highly toxic. It is prolonged pressure, worry, and frustration—resulting in chronic stress.

The Toxic Results of Chronic Stress

The contemporary business world includes enormous stress. Much of it can come from customers, clients, or one's own company in the form of increased quotas, delivery delays, pricing structure, credit policy, contests, division of territory, sales management changes, and so on.

In the selling process or any other business negotiation there is competition, rejection, industry change, time pressure, holding good customers, finding new customers, the presentation, paperwork, and getting commitment.

Salespeople, or anybody else on the payroll, must appear poised in the face of turn-down. They must appear happy to prospects when underneath there may be gnawing anxiety or, sometimes, contempt for the person they're talking with. They may harbor resentment of others who may be pressuring them to produce or "do things their way." Without release, these emotions can create a toxic condition in the body. A toxic condition can also be caused by the stress of travel, lonely evenings out of town, or the harassment of constant driving in traffic. Yet, the representative of your firm must always look fresh and sharp.

The worst forms of toxic thinking, such as intense hatreds, defeatism, pessimism, depression, and negative self-image usually don't apply to the average competent business person. As a group business people are keenly aware of the necessity of empathy with others, the positive self-image, the optimistic, winning attitude.

But to offset the toxic effects of stress mind programming is a must. It keeps one relaxed . . . keeps those toxic emotions from "getting under the skin." You very likely have the added pressure of "staying up and motivated" day in and day out. Here again, daily mind programming is an excellent way to stay enthused with high energy.

Toxic Thinking Destroys Relationships

Not only does toxic thinking produce harmful effects in the body, it produces unsatisfying or unproductive relationships with others. Such thinking affects relations with customers, prospects, employers, co-workers, spouses, children, friends, and aquaintances. Habits of negative thinking result in discontent, boredom, and apathy with job, career, marriage, or life. Such habits actually bind people, keep them from using their talents or doing the things in life they want to do. Certainly, those who hope to persuade or sell to others would find any part of toxic thinking counter productive.

Toxic Thinking Is a Killer

Most medical doctors agree that a person's attitude affects their recovery. Numerous studies have been made on how prolonged thoughts of hate, resentment, and keen disappointments in love have changed the biochemistry in the body and resulted in illness. Dr. Kenneth R. Pelletier, in his book *Mind As Healer*, says that it is now generally considered by doctors that 50 to 80 percent of all diseases are psychosomatic or stress-related.

If the uptight feeling of pressure, anxiety, and frustration goes on and on, it can trigger an oversupply of chemicals in the bloodstream that harm the body. Stressful thought patterns cause a high level of corticoids to circulate in the bloodstream, according to endocrinologist Hans Selye, one of the leaders in stress research. In time it may cause high blood pressure, damage to the kidneys, and ulcers. According to Dr. Selye, and many others exploring this field, chronic stress also causes a drop in the immune mechanisms of the T cells and the white cells. This leads to the high probability that many cancers and infectious diseases are stress-related.

Studies in absenteeism from the job have shown a definite correlation between resentment and on-the-job conflict and illness. These studies show that people who are unhappy on the job suffer from influenza more often than those who have job satisfaction.

In his book *Anatomy of an Illness,* Norman Cousins described experiments with mind control during a critical illness. Perhaps one of the most significant factors to come out of those experiments was the effect of humor on healing. Other studies have proven the great therapeutic effect of a sense of humor and of laughter in healing and in relieving stress.

Toxic Thinking Affects the Appearance

Toxic thinking is etched on the face and the body in a number of ways. Prolonged anxiety, tension, and frustration release an over-abundant supply of adrenaline. If this continues, the resulting mind patterns affect the appearance. The facial muscles sag, and body tone shows aging, as do mannerisms. It shows even in the way a person carries on a business conversation, the way they stand, sit, and move about. Add to that the toxic emotions of resentment, hatred, depression, despair, and fear and you have a sour, anxious, self-centered facial expression.

The way one thinks even affects the quickness of movement. Controlled studies of those who practiced meditation similar to the Deep Alpha method described in the previous chapter showed an increase from 0.5 to 0.3 reaction time. If you are athletically minded, this might be of interest.

Take Charge of Your Emotions

In getting into mind programming we're not suggesting you have sweet thoughts constantly. That's unrealistic. You're going to get very angry with someone at times. You're going to dislike some people, you're going to lose a good customer, you're going to get disappointed from time to time. We're talking about deeply felt resentment, hate, or loss that intensely absorbs a person's thoughts over a period of time.

We simply must guard the quality of our thinking by being constantly aware of what is negative and what is positive; what is stimulating, short-term stress and what is chronic stress. Psychologist Dr. Jim Will in his studies of daily thought processes found that 80 percent of the average person's thinking is *negative*! What a destructive menace all around us. It means we must consciously be a positive center of influence in the presence of others. We must "lift" people whenever we can. We must be ever aware of the wonderful influence of laughter and humor. Such practices and attitudes are wonderfully contagious.

Toxic thinking can keep us from achieving the kind of life we would like to have. Those constant under-the-surface, insidious little streams of negative thoughts about other people eat away at our lives and destroy our well-being, our hopes, and our dreams. One of the saddest things is that these mental put-downs of others don't make us feel better about ourselves. The critical view boomerangs on us. The negative thoughts create an uneasy feeling about our own worth. To boost the self-esteem back up we're apt to find more places to dump negatives. Thus, the cycle reinforces itself.

The person whom you don't like has fears and longings just like you. That person had no say in the decision to be on this earth, no choice in parents, no choice in genes, no choice in the critical first few years when the mass connections of the brain's neurons were taking place. Like you, that person is the most remarkable machine in the universe.

You may have good reason to dislike the acts of the person, dislike the manner, or what the person says. But for your own self-esteem, well-being, positive influence, and good health, love the person. We're all cut from the same mysterious cloth.

4

Concentration and Perception

*T*he secretary ushers you into Ken Johnson's office. In the next few minutes you will perceive a few things. If, as you walk in, you are highly anxious and concerned about what Mr. Johnson will think of you, then both your perception and your intuitive abilities will be dulled. Your concentration will be misdirected toward self. *High self-concern acts like blinders blocking out the very messages you need.*

Let's say you are reasonably well prepared for the meeting. Your company provides a service Mr. Johnson could use. You have thought through three key benefits that should influence Mr. Johnson to use your services. You have also programmed your mind on the way to the call, repeating several times, "Mr. Johnson and I will have a good, warm rapport." Following that, you have posed some key questions to yourself: "How can I help him; how can I help his company?" You have gotten out of yourself, so to speak, and set the stage for excellent perception and, perhaps, intuitive insight.

Your concentration on the surroundings lets you perceive some things. Because of the placement of Mr. Johnson's office you suspect you are dealing with someone in middle management. You wonder if he can make the decision about what you are selling.

When you first meet, he seems to have a confident, friendly manner, and talks rather freely about his company's expansion plans. Such plans would probably include a substantial amount of what you are selling. Being an excellent listener, you pick up on a few things that bother you.

You are using the "Cone of Concentration" method as you listen and observe Mr. Johnson. You are aware of the studies of how people express their feelings: The words people use actually convey only 7 percent of their true feelings; 38 percent of true feelings come through the tone of voice and the inflections; a whopping 55 percent of people's feelings are told in their eyes, lips, facial expression, and gestures.

The feedback you're getting is that Johnson's words are just that—words. You perceive that he is trying to bait you into a lower price quotation with that expansion talk. But then, some gestures aren't ringing true with that perception. He is showing apathy. Perhaps he isn't all that interested, regardless of price. You notice that he has leaned back with hands behind his neck as he talks. Now, as he listens to your presentation, his face seems to hang, his eyes are dull, he occasionally wiggles in the chair. When you show him your brochure he hardly glances at it, and the way he tosses it back on the desk indicates disinterest. Then why all this expansion discussion? Why is he subtly trying to get across the idea that he'd be placing some large orders if the price was right?

Your new perception feels right. This man is really quite insecure. He is trying to impress you with his importance. He pretended interest. His confident manner is masking something. A mix of perception and intuition has told you that dealing with Mr. Johnson could lead to a series of frustrating call-backs and put-offs and no final decision.

At that moment a large man appears in the doorway. He shoots you a glance with an "Excuse me." After a brief introduction he asks Mr. Johnson a couple of questions. The exchange certainly helps your perception. The man is questioning him about the Elkins Lake Developement. Johnson is too quick in assuring and smiling at this man. Then, after one question, Johnson's hand goes up to his face as he answers. He rubs his face a bit, then the hand goes quickly across his mouth. He also wiggles a bit, and his eyes go over to the far wall. Those are some pretty certain gestures of lying. Your "Cone of Concentration" wasn't letting anything escape.

As you listen and watch the two of them, a bit more perception surfaces. At one point Mr. Johnson is quickly relating some facts about payment terms of one of their prospects. The man in the doorway begins pursing his lips a bit and scowling slightly. Clearly, his gestures show confusion over the facts he is hearing. He is not going to buy Johnson's ideas. But Johnson doesn't read the gesture and asks his approval. The answer he gets from the man is: he'd have to think about it.

You perceived quite accurately that the man was Johnson's boss; that Johnson was afraid of him; that the man possibly did not think too much of Johnson; that Johnson probably could not make the final decision on what you were selling and that Johnson would probably lie to you. Perception as we're describing it has to do with your own experience with people or learned knowledge of how people react in various situations. However, without sharp concentration, those perceptive messages would not come through. Without that perceptive edge, you might do what the majority does: follow the line of least resistance. In this case it might be fruitless calls on Mr. Johnson.

You don't play games with yourself. Some new strategy on this prospect is in order. From your perception you know that you must call on your logic and intuition to find ways to get around Mr. Johnson without causing animosity.

THE "CONE OF CONCENTRATION"

Sharp concentration is a must for top-level selling. You must get the right feedback visually and audibly to perceive correctly. When you perceive correctly you know the benefits to outline, you know the person's probable fears and whether they are leveling with you or just trying to be nice. It doesn't matter whether you're selling a jury, selling a product or service, or selling your spouse or boss on an idea. Good perception lets you know where you stand from moment to moment.

The "Cone of Concentration" is a method that will increase that perception. All it requires is desire, mental imagery, and some practice. In radar technology the cone of vision is a term frequently used. As you stand before the radar screen, it is essential that only blips from a predetermined area be picked up. Therefore, the radar waves are sent out in the formation of a cone, eliminating all extraneous images that would clutter the screen and cause confusion over what you are receiving.

Visualizing the Cone

You can do the same with your area of concentration. Imagine, as you talk to someone, that there is a cone that goes out from your head. If you are talking to one person that cone would be just three or four feet wide, taking in the area of that person. You may wish to visualize the cone as plexiglass. The cone gets wider and smaller depending upon what you are looking at. It would be much like a television camera going for a close-up shot of one person and a wider angle for a group shot. In your next social conversation, practice imagining the cone as you talk to one person and then to a group. You are concerned only with feedback within that cone. As you imagine that cone as real and physical, you get rid of extraneous clutter. And, of course, you're fighting extraneous thoughts as you do your best to listen.

Your Fovea Vision

An important part of the concentration is your awareness of the fovea. This is a tiny area about the size of a dot located on the retina opposite your pupil. There are several hundred million light cells scattered over the retina. But at the dotlike fovea they are not scattered. That point is packed with light cells. As you read this sentence, your fovea is picking up only a few letters out of a word at a time. The rest of the retina is giving you the peripheral vision of other vague word forms.

Pupil Contact

Most of us have a tendency to let our eyes haphazardly take things in. For example, we may make eye contact with a prospect. That is not the same as pupil contact. An awareness of the fovea encourages you to concentrate where you should. A person's pupils are one of those places. I do not mean staring someone down or an attempt at intimidation. You can go from the pupil to the eyes, then to the face, and away at times. Certainly, you do not want the other person to feel uncomfortable. On the contrary, reasonable pupil contact is very complimentary; you are telling the other person that he/she is important.

Pupil contact gives you critical feedback on how a person feels about you and what you are saying. One way to know whether or not you are getting pupil contact is to ask yourself after you leave a person, "What color eyes does he or she have?" If you remember the color, you have undoubtedly made beautiful contact. Ask yourself that a few times, and it will remind you to look into the pupils.

Feedback from the Lips

Another critical fovea contact point of vision is the person's lips. Watch how they change, get tight, part a bit, purse. Lips tell a great deal about how a person is reacting to you. Practice this socially by observing lip reactions to what one person is saying to another.

Listening

Use the "Cone of Concentration" as you listen. To listen well is not easy. For example, in a restaurant as you're trying to talk with a customer or prospect, if it isn't loud music, it's poor acoustics and reverberating chatter that interfere with your ability to listen. Also, most people are sloppy with their speech. They mumble, ramble, run words together, or enunciate poorly. The image of the cone will help gather in the words.

Here are four steps to excellent listening:

1. Face the person.
2. Get pupil contact.
3. Be involved, nod, smile, or comment.
4. Hang on every word that is said.

That last one is the toughest. The concentration span of an adult averages between one and eight seconds. You want to stretch that as much as possible. We tend to skip hither and yon in our thoughts as we half listen to someone. One of the reasons is that we are thinking so much faster than the talking speed of the other person. We may be thinking 400 to 700 words a minute while the talking speed of the person we're with may be 120 words a minute. The cone idea keeps that fast thinking centered on feedback from the object.

For just five days, thirty minutes a day, practice those four steps with anyone you're talking with. Imagine the cone idea as you listen. At the end of five days your perception and concentration will be markedly increased. You will hear inflections you hadn't been aware of before. You will catch the subtle truths behind words.

Body Language

As noted above, only a small part of our feelings come across with words. To perceive a person's reactions, we must concentrate mostly on the feedback we're getting from the tone of voice, inflection, the eyes, facial expression and the gestures. Apart from the eyes, lips, and voice, the isolated gesture might be misleading. Therefore, it is important to observe clusters of gestures that seem to tie in with one another. Here are five clusters of body language from my book *The Psychology of Closing Sales* (published by Prentice-Hall, Inc.)

Rejection. The arms might be folded. That wouldn't tell you much unless you also noticed a clenched fist or a touching of the side of the nose. Other important signals are shoulders at an angle to you, tight lips, eyes cold, possibly drifting away from yours. If standing, the person may back away. Voice is probably flat. Probably gives short answers.

Indifference. This attitude is common. It's particularly common where buyers are seeing many salespeople every day. And this is understandable. They have to sit through many insufferably boring presentations. After many years of this they just don't get all that excited when another salesperson walks in the door.

I like to call this cluster the "hangs." When a person is bored or indifferent the muscles of the face literally hang. A person looks ten years older with the "hangs." If the prospect shows this, you'll probably also notice a haggard look around the eyes. He may squirm occasionally in the chair, or tap the desk, or lean back with his hands behind his neck. There may be little response to your questions. If standing, the prospect probably won't get too close. Any two or three of these would be a "cluster," and your diagnosis would likely be accurate.

Lying. The following gestures are not 100 percent accurate, but the percentage of accuracy is high. As in the example above with Mr. Johnson, a person might say something, then, at the same time, the hand would come up to the face and possibly cross the mouth or rub the side of the face or a lip. The person might also squirm in the chair, or if standing, shift the weight. The eyes will usually turn away or down from yours.

Confusion. In the middle of your presentation you may perceive a slight scowl, a pursing of the mouth, or, perhaps, a puzzled look. Quite possibly you have said something that the prospect does not understand. Remember the ego; nobody wants to appear stupid. I have seen this cluster many times as I have sat in on sales presentations. I've seen it frequently when the salesperson went too fast in covering the terms and conditions of a contract. It can frequently be spotted when a salesperson is too glib with words such as modem, buffer, rom and ram in the computer business, or demographic terminology in marketing.

Interest. The prospect might show a liking toward you or what you're saying, or both. He may start with a mildly interested look, perhaps leaning back in his chair. As interest grows, he may lean forward and face you directly. Eyes seem to sparkle and show animation, and the prospect looks at you frequently. If you're both standing, he may move closer. His voice sounds interested and he responds easily to your questions. He may even nod his head. You're getting buying signals. It's time to close.

Cutting Clutter

The more you cut clutter the more your "Cone of Concentration" is enhanced. Clutter can be a messy desk, room, car, purse, briefcase, or files. Clutter can be people's distractions, demands, and constant interruptions. Clutter can be the noise pollution of radio, television, so-called background music, endless chatter of those around us, and booming, overbearing or strident voices of individuals.

As one sharpens concentration, perception is increased. The more perception, the more intuition. One seems to blend into the other, as you will see in the next chapter. The magic of this threesome—concentration, perception, and intuition—will steer you well in influencing your course of action with others.

5

Intuition

Coupled with sound logic, intuition is the cybernetic guidance system to making the right calls on the right people at the right time. Intuitive insight can make the difference between one more ordinary presentation and a brilliant display that moves people to action. Intuition gives you ideas on dress, manner, what to ask and how to ask it, how to get commitment, and how to work hand in glove with your own company to get the most cooperation. It is a wonderful, mysterious force at your disposal. We're going to explore ways to enhance that force in your work and in your life.

The intuitive process applies to any new or unique idea on how to get a raise, get a job, sell your ideas to someone, solve a marketing problem, solve a people problem, make an investment, or choose a mate. In many cases a breakthrough idea is both perception and intuition. For example, an idea seems to come out of nowhere, but actually, back in the recesses of the mind, there was a learned experience. However, the application of that idea may be a new twist and totally intuitive.

WHAT IS INTUITION?

Around the world, physicists, psychologists, neuropsychologists, and parapsychologists are working on that question. Great strides have been made in how it seems to work. What it is, no one knows exactly. A reporter once asked Thomas Edison what electricity was. Edison replied, "I don't know, but use it." We all experience intuition in "hunches" and "feelings." Intuition may come in quiet whispers or nagging nudges. We can, and should, encourage it, develop it, expect it, and lean on it. It is the wellspring of ideas. It can also be an innovative way to handle a person, an exciting new way to make a presentation, or a novel approach to solving a problem. Intuition is your own private springboard, bouncing you to new levels in your career and life. It can't be forced or pressured for answers. Rather, it must be quietly wooed.

Most scientists now agree that intuition is a fantastic tool that can quickly cut through to the truth. Albert Einstein said there is no logical road to natural laws . . . only intuition. Many scientists and physicists see intuition as universal vibration waves. Stanford neuropsychologist Karl Pribram opened the door with his very plausible holograph speculation: Certain outside waves that correlate with our particular interests set up a resonance with our own brain waves. They mesh much like the light wave principle in three-dimensional holography. This may be one explanation of why identical ideas of inventors and creative people frequently surface within days or weeks of each other.

The use of intuition by business leaders is out of the closet. For years only logic and facts were the things respected. Many of the country's leaders found themselves in the position of deciding intuitively and then finding the facts to back up their positions. Henry Mintzberg reported on a study of executives in the Jan./Feb. 1981 issue of the *Harvard Business Review*. The finding was that the thought processes and decisions of most corporate leaders were a blend of logic and powerful intuition.

Intuition is a very effective and serious business tool. In the field of high-level selling it is a must. Studies of intuitive people show them to be more alert, poised, highly independent, and self-confident. In my opinion some of the most intuitive people, as a group, are salespeople. To be effective, they must rely on a constant stream of intuitive insights in overcoming obstacles.

Five Kinds of Intuition

Psychologist, Philip Goldberg, in his excellent book, *The Intuitive Edge* (published by Jeremy P. Tarcher, Inc.), outlines various types of intuition: Discovery, Creative, Evaluation, Operation, and Prediction. Some people are intuitive in one area, some in a number or all of them. To help you recognize intuitive insight and how it can be applied, here are examples of each of the types in selling.

Discovery Intuition. Frequently this comes as a flash of insight. This happened to Dick Stockton as he and his wife sat quietly in a yogurt parlor in Belleview, Washington.

"I've got it," he said.

"Got what?" asked his wife, surprised at the outburst.

"Write-on calendars!"

"What do you mean, 'write-on calendars'?"

"Those big, five-foot-wide plastic calendars that companies put on walls. Businesses use them to write production schedules or vacation schedules."

"Uh huh."

"Well, Jacobs is going to go with a different specialty company this year unless I can come up with a promotional gift that's unique, and stays under $14 each. He's got fifty-three hundred dealers.

"Now, here's my idea. Each dealer would get one of those huge write-on calendars, which they'd love and use. And at the bottom of some of those date spaces we could put little reminders about certain seasonal items coming up that they should be ordering or reordering. The reminders would stare them in their faces for a whole year. It's a natural!"

Dick Stockton netted $28,000 on the intuitive idea.

Creative Intuition. Laura Atkins, owner of her own travel agency, contracted for a booth in a large bridal show promotion. She was hoping to pick up prospective honeymoon business to faraway places. The problem was, which of hundreds of posters should she put up in the small, ten-foot booth space? How could she make her booth stand out among all the exhibitors? As she was driving, the idea hit her.

Forget the usual honeymoon spots. Display one dramatic picture of a cruise ship. Stage the large picture and the entire booth with beautiful flowers, soft lighting, and warm colors. Logically, the cruise ship idea didn't make sense since most of her cruise business had been with middle-aged couples, not honeymooners. But her intuition told her the display would have exciting honeymoon appeal. It drew the biggest crowd, and resulted in an exceptional day of cruise bookings. Her intuition was right on target.

Evaluative Intuition. One of the problems in the corporate structure is that you're expected to explain a decision logically. That happened to Chester Tellepsen after he submitted a sealed bid to an oil company on a string of pipelines. Production and management had decided on a bid of $3,282,327. They were happy with it, but Chester wasn't. He had a strong hunch they had made an error somewhere in the analysis.

That evening he went out to dinner with his wife.

"Mary, the quote's wrong. . . . I know it's wrong. It's just not going to fly at that price. I got a feeling Hank's estimate on hauling the pipe was too high."

"But the quote's already been sent," Mary answered.

"I know, but I've got a feeling we can still get that order. I'm going to call Martin."

"But it's 10:30 P.M. You know he's always in bed by 9:30 P.M."

Chester called his boss, told him he knew this was most unusual, but he'd like to put another bid in. He agreed that all the figures seemed in line, but he had a strong feeling that there had been an error somewhere . . . that he wanted to go in at $3,264,320.

His boss said they could live with that, to go ahead if he felt that strongly. They got the order. A competitor came close with $3,268,500. That intuition about the cost of transporting the pipe proved correct. They had figured the wrong contractual rate.

Although intuition paid off in this case, there are hazards in this kind of insight. What one thinks is "intuitive insight" could actually be strong emotional desire. It simply means we have to be careful in evaluating what emotions are involved.

Operative Intuition. In this, one feels "drawn" to something. It could be a strong feeling about a new career. It may be doing something in a different way. That's what happened to Ray Atkins. This example is taken from my book *Psychology of Closing Sales.* Ray sold time for a radio station that had only fair listener numbers. The top buyer for a large meat packer was coming to town to place budgets with a few select radio stations.

Each station representative was to present his or her story to the buyer in a hotel room. Every thirty minutes the buyer would listen to the pitch of a different rep. My friend realized he didn't have a chance in this kind of comparative buying and would somehow have to present his story in a unique style. He bought a woman's purse at Sear's and put a typed note inside which said:

> We have a big female audience in the twenty-one to forty-nine age bracket. Seventy percent of our audience is female

. . . they buy meat products, and we'd like to tell them about
your fine meats.

Then he had the purse with the message sent to the hotel room
by a bellman. The buyer thought it was the most unique presentation he had ever seen. He placed an annual budget with the station,
eliminating four competitive stations with the same music format.

Ray dared to be different. He took a risk. The buyer might have
been offended at getting a purse . . . or maybe he wouldn't have
liked the deviation from the structured presentation format. But, as
Ray said, "I knew the idea was right when it hit me. I couldn't wait
to do it!"

Predictive Intuition. Ann Sheldon "just knew" that if she could
talk with the chief executive officer of a large mail order firm in
New Jersey she could get their paper business. Their present supplier had a lock on the business for the past four years. She couldn't
get through the various screens to get an appointment with the
CEO. So she called the head of accounting and got the names of
possible "influencers" and the CEO. Each received a wire that she
would be arriving at 10:00 A.M. the next day and that she would like
to meet with them briefly regarding their paper costs.

The next morning she was at the desk of the chief executive
officer. He was in a meeting but had left word that she see the head
buyer. She asked his secretary if she could possibly wait, that she
just wanted to meet the CEO. In about thirty minutes he came in.
His secretary explained that Ann Sheldon wanted to meet him for
just a few minutes. They went into his office. He asked questions. It
was more than a brief courtesy meeting. He had his secretary call
in the buyer and head of production. They asked her a few questions.

Then the CEO asked a strange question. "Ann, do you have any
idea how many paper companies are after our business?"

"I imagine a lot of them," she answered with a smile.

"Well, you couldn't have made a sales call at a better time.
Yesterday we discovered that for over a year our supplier has been
padding the bills. We let them go this morning. Ann, I've been
impressed with your answers." He turned to the others. "What do
you think? Unless either of you think otherwise, let's give her
company a chance."

Coincidence, perhaps, that she arrived just as they were dumping another vendor. But why the sudden strong "feeling" on her part? That's predictive intuition.

Steps to Stimulate Intuition

Certain things stimulate more intuition. Doing those things will give you a great edge. There are also factors to be wary of. Let's start with the positive.

Incubation. Frequently, intuitive insights are instantaneous. There is no incubation period. Perhaps you get a flash of direction or sense that a person is not dependable. But for problems or major decisions, or how to handle something, an incubation period seems to work best. When possible sleep on the idea or problem, or do something that will get your mind on something else.

A number of scientists have speculated on some probable reasons for this. They believe it may have to do with forming new neurotransmitters in the brain's neurons; that as you concentrate on a problem, a particular amino acid molecular string is formed. This takes a bit of time. Then these new neurotransmitters have to traverse down the neuron axon, where they are fired across synaptic gaps to other neurons. Somehow these thoughts resonate with incoming wave vibrations or resonate with related facts and ideas in your brain. You emerge with a new insight. By not forcing it, by pursuing something else, you give it time and do not block the incredible activity going on in your brain.

All this may seem a bit far out. However, research has confirmed the wave vibration of thought. Fascinating experiments regarding intuition and thought are going on in major universities throughout the world. Intuition is a marvelous guidance tool for effective selling. Therefore, I believe it is important to bring in the physiology and what is scientifically presumed to take place in the brain. It is included in this book simply to lend verification and credibility to what many already sense to be true.

Intuitive Reception. It is important to know the actual places where you are most receptive to intuitive ideas. Just being aware of those places will increase the flow of messages. And oh how quickly they come and go as fleeting whispers across the mind. Be careful you don't trample these little sprouts with the indifferent heel of logical, overriding thoughts.

Research has pinpointed a number of locations or activities where intuition seems to thrive. These seem to be the most popular: shower or bath, driving, shaving, gardening, jogging, walking, lying in bed, eating alone, or working on some project. As you read that list, you probably identified one or more locations where you seem to get ideas. That very recognition will increase your intuitive flow.

Expectancy. Instruct your subconscious mind that you expect an answer. You are not trying to force it, you simply have the faith that it will be there. This is excellent practice while in a meditative state or just as you are drifting off to sleep. You simply state the problem and request the subconscious mind to work out the correct solution. If worries ever keep you awake at night try this "unloading" technique.

Early-Morning Message. During your first waking moments ask your subconscious if you have any messages. It is a little like going to a Telex machine or your computer for electronic mail except what you're asking for are intuitive insights of any kind that may help you. Here's a suggestion on what to say to yourself as you awaken.

"This is going to be a wonderful, interesting day. What messages do you have for me this morning?" Then wait a minute or two. Now, you're not going to hear voices, and much of the time there will be nothing. Also, if something does cross your mind, it may not be intuitive at all, simply a reminder of something you have to do that day. But among the chaff there may be an excellent idea on how to handle something, what to do, whom to talk to, where to go. The practice is so simple. Make it a morning habit. If this appeals to you, take a moment right now to instruct your mind: "Each morning, starting with tomorrow, I will ask for messages as soon as I awaken. I am now programming this into my memory."

Checklist for Selling and Persuasion

You will definitely close more and larger sales by using a two-minute mental checklist as you prepare to make a sales call, or any business presentation. You simply pose questions to your subconscious mind and wait for answers and ideas. Move from question to question, allowing a little time after each question for an answer to surface. Do not be concerned if no answer is immediately forthcoming. Frequently, the answer bubbles through a little later, after you've run through the list.

You'll get some excellent direction. Some of it will be logic, some of it intuitive. Most of it will be a mix of the two. Better presentations will be immediately apparent. You might want to clip the list to the sun visor of your car where it can easily be checked. If you prefer, go over the list before leaving your office or in a parking area at your final destination. Here are the questions. Say them outloud or silently, as you prefer:

1. Which benefits will help this person?
2. Exactly how will those benefits help?
3. What unique, imaginative idea can I present to this person?
4. What does this person probably want . . . personally?
5. Is this person afraid of someone?
6. Can this person make the final decision?
7. Who else might influence the decision?
8. If this isn't the decision-maker how can I get to the right person?
9. What are the *real* objections this person may have?
10. How should I handle them?
11. What three testimonial stories can I use in closing?
12. How will I ask for the business?

Brainstorm

Use this where you want to come up with a plan or an idea. For example, "How can I increase my sales?" Use a tape recorder, get comfortable, pose the question out loud. Let yourself go with any idea that crosses your mind, however ridiculous. Do not let yourself get one bit judgmental about anything you say. One crazy idea may lead to another.

Set yourself a time limit, say five minutes, possibly ten. Just keep coming up with ideas, no matter how outlandish. When you're through take a short break before playing the tape. You're allowing a bit of incubation time. Now play the tape and evaluate. Most of the ideas will be worthless. You're looking for that jewel of an idea. If it isn't right there on the tape, that short incubation time may let something you put on the tape trigger the "eureka" idea.

Use this for your stream of problems: What visual would be most effective? How can I get around that price objection? How can I get around Susan Smith to Don Schwartz without offending Susan Smith? How can I help my manager and thus help myself?

Don't be impatient or discouraged if, at times, no worthwhile ideas come forth.

Word Diagram

On a sheet of paper put down a word or state an objective. Circle it. From that, connect other ideas. For example, from the circle "How to increase sales," you may wish to put down the idea, "Make more calls." Circle that and connect it with a line to the circle with "How to increase sales." Connecting to "Make more calls" you may have a number of circles such as, "Get up list of fifty high-potential prospects," "Set aside Tuesday mornings and Thursday mornings only for new calls." A connecting one might be "Find time for new calls." Hooked on to that could be "Come to office earlier," "Do paperwork after 4:40 P.M., "Cut long coffee breaks," "Service small accounts more by phone."

Though much of the word diagram will be logical, you'll find some excellent intuitive solutions flowing in.

Sometimes a seemingly intuitive insight will turn out poorly. As you act on intuition this will happen, but it shouldn't discourage you. Most of your true intuitions will be correct, so allow for error. Also, keep in mind that what might seem like misguided intuition may lead you into something quite wonderful in a very unforeseen way.

Intuition flourishes where there is an open mind and carefree attitude. It seems to thrive where there is a light touch, a sense of humor, and no taking oneself too seriously. It is a beautiful gift to be used and cherished.

6

Your Personality Style

*D*ave Arnold sat down at his desk after Steve Jackson, the micro-film salesman, left. What was it about that man that bothered him? The chain bracelet? Maybe. Steve knew he was turned off by show-offs or pretentious people . . . or people who exaggerated. And Steve did stretch the claims of his product a bit.

Maybe what he didn't like was Steve's insensitivity when he laid his presentation book on the desk. He almost pushed the gold-framed picture of Dave's two daughters off onto the floor.

Mr. Arnold had all the traits of the *S* or Solid type personality. These are the Jimmy Stewart types, the warm, mature, sincere people of the world. They're family oriented, care deeply about friends, and frequently keep in touch with old school chums. People who try to sell them find they won't be pushed. Although they seem laid back, they can be quite stubborn and are not easily manipulated.

In his role as chief executive officer of Pangor Instruments, Mr. Arnold has built a reputation of quality products and employee performance. Growth is steady and solid, always maintaining highest integrity standards with every Pangor customer.

One hundred miles away, Doc Street paced next to his desk as he carried on a conference-call hook-up with three of his managers. Five years earlier Doc was one of Pangor's top salespeople, then left to open up his own medical instruments business called Skilmed, Incorporated. Big changes were happening in the medical field. Hospitals and clinics were suddenly being run like businesses, with heavy emphasis on marketing and cost effectiveness. Doc Street latched onto the new opportunities.

He worked fifteen hours a day expanding Skilmed into six cities across the country. Actually these "branch offices" were simply phone-answering services in six executive suites. But the appearance of a few well-placed full-page ads was the leverage he needed to cut some good buying arrangements with various product manufacturers.

Five years later he had a nationwide sales force of sixty-four people. His ambitious expansion was built on volume and lower prices. Services to his customers were spread very thin. So were his finances. Doc Street was playing a risky game. Still, in this short time he was making inroads into some of Pangor's better accounts.

Doc is a *D* or Dominant personality type. He is a restless person who wants action right now. At this moment, on the phone with his managers, he was interrupting with his opinions on how something should have been handled. He wasn't the best listener, which, at times, would exasperate some of his people. He had little patience with those who didn't get to the point quickly. Some wondered why he continually drove himself. Actually, this ego drive of power and competition wasn't work. It was his hobby, his greatest satisfaction.

Dave Arnold tried to call his wife Janice one more time. The phone was still busy. This was his third try in forty-five minutes. Who could she be talking to? Probably some friend. She had plenty of them. Sometimes those phone conversations would go on forever. Janice was an *E* or Expressive personality type.

It was Janice who kept the social calendar moving: inviting the Drakes for dinner, making arrangements with two other couples to see a musical, or setting up a tennis date. Sometimes the arrangements weren't what Dave Arnold wanted, but he patiently went along with them. Actually, he secretly admired her ability with people. She always seemed to have enthusiasm, and a special lilt in her voice as she talked. Sometimes he would be amused as she nodded her head and seemed to listen. Frequently her thoughts were miles away.

Each morning she would make a long "to do" list. It always made her feel so organized. In reality, she was quite disorganized. Her natural optimism made her feel there was time to "squeeze" in one more thing. But if her time management wasn't the best, her humor, trust, and interest in people made up for it.

Janice liked the "good" life: fine surroundings, clothes, the "in" places to eat. She loved a challenge if it was a mix of interesting people, variety, and a good cause. As one of the leaders in the United Fund, she did an excellent job in getting local TV personalities to make appearances at the large companies in the area.

Dave tried the phone again and gave up with a sigh. He had wanted to let Janice know he'd be late. He didn't want to rush the interview with Karen Carter. And he still had to put together the points of the plan that he'd present to the board tomorrow.

Outside his office, Karen was beginning to feel a bit down. Why was Mr. Arnold letting her sit out there so long? It had been ten minutes since that salesman came out of his office. Maybe this was Mr. Arnold's way of letting her know he wouldn't consider her for that new position she wanted so much. Now she was a bit mad at herself for thinking negatively. But Karen Carter couldn't help analyzing everything. She was an *A* or Analytical personality type.

"I'm sorry, Karen. Didn't mean to keep you sitting out here so long." Mr. Arnold was standing in his doorway. His warm sincerity lifted her spirits immediately. "Come on in," he said.

"Thank you." She smiled and took the chair over to the side, rather than across the desk from him. Karen knew herself well. She was a bit shy outwardly, but she had strong feelings about what she wanted. Taking a chair away from any desk barrier was part of her assertive planning for this interview. Besides, she looked professional and trim. Why not make the most of it by taking the chair at the side?

Mr. Arnold settled in his chair with his hands clasped together. He looked right at Karen. She met his gaze, smiled slightly, and came right to the point. She didn't feel very comfortable with small talk and didn't like to play games.

"Mr. Arnold, I understand that you are looking for someone to supervise and develop training programs." Karen paused. She was trying to choose her words carefully. "I would like to be considered for that position."

Dave Arnold squirmed a bit, looked down at his desk, then explained the position and type of person he was seeking. As he talked he realized he had almost "conditioned" himself that he was looking for a man to fill the position. It would require some special talents since they were just adding dianoetic instruments and programs to their line.

Without pushing, Karen carefully called his attention to her background and accomplishments at the company, including supervising their transition to computers, screening engineering and technical applicants, her excellent presentation to a visiting hospital staff when marketing specialist, Mr. Embry, was ill.

Karen Carter was well organized, neat, and soft-spoken. Inside she was a nervous wreck. But she knew she was coming across with poise. Her sharp intuition told her she had sold Mr. Arnold. She had all her "credits" neatly itemized on a sheet of paper just in case Mr. Arnold wanted to look it over. He did.

"May I have this?" he asked. His eyes sparkled a bit. He smiled. "I'll let you know tomorrow, and, Karen, thanks for coming in."

There is a little of these people in every one of us. Each person is a unique combination of four basic behavior styles, according to the late psychologist, William M. Marston. A person's behavioral style very accurately shows up in the instrument called the DESAnalysis.* The DESAnalysis on the following pages is based on Marston's studies (published in *Emotions of Normal People*, Persona Press, Inc.) and is the result of five years of adaptation by your author.

Working with a set of twenty-two word groups, you will very quickly pinpoint the characteristics of your own behavior or personality style. It graphically reveals your persuasive strengths in dealing with others. It guides you in using those strengths more effectively.

You will gain an insight into the reactions of other people. The DESAnalysis targets the clues that help you "read" the probable behavior style of another person. Awareness of a person's inner feelings and how they will probably react gives you a distinct advantage in persuading that person to do what you want them to do.

You also become more alert to a possible weakness in your own style of persuasion and can objectively offset it. For example, an outgoing, talkative person may be quite friendly, but a possible weakness would be talking right past the point of trying to get a commitment from the other person.

The DESAnalysis is not a test in the sense that you could flunk it or score poorly. The results are neither good nor bad. There is no "best" style or type. You will simply choose certain words that seem most like you and words that seem least like you. You'll then plot the results on the **DESA GRAPH** to graphically see your pattern or personality style.

---

* The copyrighted DESAnalysis is included here, in part, by permission of Patton Communications, Inc., 3000 Wilcrest, Houston, Texas 77042. The five-page DESAnalysis, explaining the various combinations of styles plus instructions in using it in team building and screening is available in quantity orders.

Your personality, the way you think, influence, and react to people and situations will show on the DESA GRAPH in the relationship between these four behavior styles:

D   Your DOMINANT behavior
E   Your EXPRESSIVE behavior
S   Your SOLID behavior
A   Your ANALYTICAL behavior

Use a pen or a pencil to select your word choices. The total time will be between ten to twenty minutes.

Proceed as quickly as possible. Be as objective as you can. Do not be concerned if some of the words are not exactly on target or whether you've answered every one exactly right. It's almost impossible to be completely honest in any self-analysis. The DESAnalysis is "weighted" to take this into consideration.

MARKING INSTRUCTIONS

1. In each of the four word groups, choose one word that is most like you. Mark it with an *X* in the MOST column. (Disregard the small letters in the boxes.) *Choose only one word* even though you feel more than one word "is most" like you. See the example.
2. Next, in each four-word group, *choose just one word* that least describes you and mark it with an *X* in the LEAST column.
3. In choosing the one word in MOST and LEAST, try to think of how you react at work rather than at home or socially with close friends (unless you want to see how you are socially). Do not choose the words you think a spouse or friend would choose. Choose how *you* feel. And remember, you cannot possibly do poorly. There is no "best" in behavioral styles.

EXAMPLE

	MOST	LEAST
BLUNT		X
TALKATIVE		
SYSTEMATIC	X	
DETAILED		

	MOST	LEAST		MOST	LEAST
INTENSE	D	D	IMPATIENT	D	D
EXACTING	A	A	PARTICULAR	A	A
OPEN AND CHATTY	E	E	STIMULATING	E	E
COMFORTABLE	S	S	THOUGHTFUL	S	S
EMOTIONAL	E	E	WELL-LIKED	E	E
ORGANIZED	A	A	THOROUGH	A	A
DOMINEERING	D	D	COMPETITIVE	D	D
POISED	S	S	KIND-HEARTED	S	S
HELPFUL	S	S	WELL PREPARED	A	A
BLUNT	D	D	SELF-ASSURED	D	D
MODEST	A	A	UNDERSTANDING	S	S
OUT-GOING	E	E	BRIGHT OUTLOOK	E	E
COMPLIANT	A	A	FULL OF LIFE	E	E
FORCEFUL	D	D	AMBITIOUS	D	D
RELAXED	S	S	RATIONAL	A	A
APPEALING	E	E	WILLING	S	S
CAUTIOUS	S	S	ENTERPRISING	D	D
FUN-LOVING	E	E	ENTHUSIASTIC	E	E
FACTUAL	A	A	PERFECTIONIST	A	A
UNYIELDING	D	D	RELIABLE	S	S
DIPLOMATIC	A	A	ACCURATE	A	A
DRIVING	D	D	GOOD LISTENER	S	S
COMPOSED	S	S	ENTERTAINING	E	E
MAGNETIC	E	E	SINGLE-MINDED	D	D
CAREFUL	A	A	ANIMATED	E	E
AFFECTIONATE	S	S	LOYAL	S	S
STYLISH	E	E	SYSTEMATIC	A	A
STRIVING	D	D	FORWARD	D	D
TACTFUL	A	A	SENSITIVE	A	A
CONSIDERATE	S	S	FRIENDLY	S	S
SPONTANEOUS	E	E	DEFINITENESS	D	D
STRONG-WILLED	D	D	SOCIALIZER	E	E
ENERGETIC	D	D	CORRECT	A	A
SPARKLING	E	E	AGGRESSIVE	D	D
WARM	S	S	SYMPATHETIC	S	S
RESPECTFUL	A	A	RESPONSIVE	E	E

	MOST	LEAST		MOST	LEAST
METICULOUS	A	A	GIVING	S	S
HEADSTRONG	D	D	VIVACIOUS	E	E
LIGHT-HEARTED	E	E	VIGOROUS	D	D
POSSESSIVE	S	S	COURTEOUS	A	A
EFFICIENT	A	A	DEMANDING	D	D
INFLUENCER	E	E	DEMONSTRATIVE	E	E
INITIATOR	D	D	LAID-BACK	S	S
COMPANIONABLE	S	S	SELF-DISCIPLINED	A	A

SCORING INSTRUCTIONS

1. Now, count all the *X* marks that fall on a letter *D* in the **MOST** columns. Enter the total in the score box next to D and under **MOST**. (In each four-word group, you should have marked just one word.)
2. Next, count all the *X* marks that fall on the letter *D* in the **LEAST** columns. Enter the total in the score box next to *D* and under **LEAST**. (In each word group, you should have marked just one word.)
3. Do the same for *E, S,* and *A.*
4. Subtract the **LEAST** from the **MOST** to get the **RESULT**. Some results will show a minus. For example, if you had a 3 in the *D* under **MOST** and an 8 under **LEAST**, you would subtract the 8 from the 3, leaving a **RESULT** of minus 5. (Rarely will there be all pluses or all minuses.)

	MOST	LEAST	RESULT
D			
E			
S			
A			

PLOTTING INSTRUCTIONS

Now take the figures from the RESULT column of the scorebox and find those figures on the DESA GRAPH. Fill in the rectangular box where that number falls under the *D, E, S,* and *A* (see the example). The highest bar on the DESA GRAPH that you have marked is your key behavioral style. Any others that also fall in the white area of the graph indicate strong behavior of that particular style. Any rectangular bar that you marked in the gray area indicates a passive or opposite behavior.

The higher the markings in the white area, the greater the intensity of that influence. Usually, if there is a very high marking in the white area of the graph, there will also be a very low marking in the gray area. Do not be concerned if any markings are off the graph—in either direction.

Chances are you have more than one marking in the white area. You will be a blend of some of the descriptions on the following pages.

D	E	S	A
18	15	17	13
17	14	16	12
16	13	14	11
15	12	13	10
14	11	12	9
13	10	11	8
12	9	10	7
		■	
11			6
10	8	8	5
9	7	7	4
8		6	3
7	6	5	■
		4	
6	5	3	1
5		2	0
4	4	1	−1
3		0	−2
2	3	−1	−3
1	2	−2	−4
0	1	−3	−5
−1			−6
		−4	−7
■			
−3	0	−5	
	−1	−6	
−4	−2		−8
−5	−3	−7	
−6			
−7		−8	−9
−8	−4	−9	−10
	■		
−9			−11
−10		−10	
	−6		−12
		−11	
−11	−7		
−12	−8		−13
−13	−9	−12	−14

D	E	S	A
18	15	17	13
17	14	16	12
16	13	14	11
15	12	13	10
14	11	12	9
13	10	11	8
12	9	10	7
		9	
11			6
10	8	8	5
9	7	7	4
8		6	3
7	6	5	2
		4	
6	5	3	1
5		2	0
4	4	1	−1
3		0	−2
2	3	−1	−3
1	2	−2	−4
0	1	−3	−5
−1			−6
		−4	−7
−2			
−3	0	−5	
	−1	−6	
−4	−2		−8
−5	−3	−7	
−6			
−7		−8	−9
−8	−4	−9	−10
	−5		
−9			−11
−10		−10	
	−6		−12
		−11	
−11	−7		
−12	−8		−13
−13	−9	−12	−14

D OR DOMINANT STYLE

If your *D* is high in the white area of the **DESA GRAPH**, you will probably show most of the following traits as you react with people. If your *D* is anywhere in the white area, you will certainly exhibit many of these traits:

Like the challenge of accomplishment
Task oriented rather than people oriented
Like power and prestige
Restless and apt to be impatient
Decisive
Can be impulsive
Frequently want to change things
Usually quite direct, may be abrupt
Can argue one minute and laugh the next
Not the best listener, may interrupt
Have high ego
May lack empathy (unless there is also *S* or *E* in white area)
Quick and direct
Like to juggle many tasks or interests at once
Desk is frequently messy (unless the *A* is strong)
Too impatient to wait in line (two people is a long line)
If your *D* is extremely high it would show arrogance.

If you are a salesperson:

Enjoy the challenge of selling
Want results now
No problem making cold calls or trying to close
Very competitive
Probably like sales contests
Want freedom from control by others
May give manager fits on policy or getting reports in
Possible weaknesses could be impatience
Another could be too little preparation before a call

If you are on the buying side:

Want to get to the point with a minimum of small talk
Quickly find out if salesperson knows his business

Apt to cut interview short
Want to get to the bottom line quickly
Don't like "mealymouthed" people
Can't take laborious details
Expect salesperson to close
Being impatient, you may interrupt
Probably decisive and possibly impulsive.

E *OR EXPRESSIVE STYLE*

If your *E* is high in the white area of the DESA GRAPH, you will probably show most of the following traits as you react with people. If your *E* is anywhere in the white area, you will certainly exhibit many of these traits:

Very spontaneous and friendly
Animated and entertaining
People oriented
Very confident
High degree of ego
Enjoy talking: expressive in speech and gestures
Quite trusting and may be lenient
Like social and business recognition and prestige
Like the "good life" and elegant atmosphere
Probably live up to income unless there is a strong *S* or *A* present
Optimistic, not too concerned with tomorrow
Dislike writing out reports or filling out forms
May be disorganized unless there is a strong *S* or *A*
Prefer making a report in person
Restless: like change, variety, anything new and different
Time management is biggest problem, organizing self and work
Closets and drawers can be a mess (unless there is high *S* or *A*)

If you are a salesperson:

No fear in making cold calls
Make a good first impression
Every call, in a way, is a social event
Friendly and articulate

Instinctively know how to make a good presentation
Enthusiastic and emotional
Weakness can be tendency to "wing it"
May talk beyond point where buyer is ready to close
May be late with reports

If you are on the buying side:

Friendly, enthusiastic, and emotional
May look for status symbols in a product or service
Like new ideas, new approaches, new products and services
Dislike slow, boring, too-detailed presentations
Frequently follow your emotions in buying
Enjoy showmanship
May be impressed by prestigious testimonials
May only appear to be listening
Like to be entertained at "in" places

S OR SOLID STYLE

If your *S* is high in the white area of the **DESA GRAPH,** you will
probably show most of the following traits as you react with people.
If your *S* is anywhere in the white area, you will certainly exhibit
many of these traits:

Most mature of the four types
Very sincere with a quiet warmth
The best listener
Friendly manner
High and steady performer, great team player
Give loyalty and expect it in return
Feel deeply, but usually hold in emotions
Modest, unassuming, and patient
Dependable and responsible
Logical: like a structured approach in reaching decisions
Seemingly easygoing but can be stubborn when pressured
Care deeply about family and friends
Do not like sudden changes in job, location, friends
Concerned about security and good performance
Have strong friendships, socially or at work

Cross you once and it will never be forgotten
Do not care for show-offs or pretentious people
Of the four types, you work best with all others
Very supportive of others or a cause
Great integrity

If you are a salesperson:

Tops with customers because of service and concern
Good understanding of customers' problems
Tough for competition to dislodge
Best at developing long-term customers
Low-key salesperson, but very persistent
Integrity: must be proud of own company's standards
May spend too much time servicing at expense of new calls
Not best for the one-call close, such as door to door
Makes friends out of prospects and customers

If you are on the buying side:

You gauge a salesperson by integrity and loyalty
Cautious and mature in reaching a buying decision
Usually will not buy on first call
Like specifics rather than generalizations
Lie to you once and that salesperson is through forever
Once you buy, you place great trust in the salesperson's word
Quiet, relaxed, dress conservatively, excellent listener
Sincere, warm, and friendly
Won't be pushed or manipulated; can be quite stubborn
Can't stand overly dramatic show-offs

A OR ANALYTICAL STYLE

If your *A* is high in the white area of the DESA GRAPH, you will probably show most of the following traits as you react with people. If your *A* is anywhere in the white area, you will certainly exhibit many of these traits:

Rarely bluffed
Mind is like a steel trap

Strive for perfection in everything you do
Like to plan and prepare well
Excellent at solving problems
Worry about things and therefore like back-up solutions
Sensitive to criticism and abhor making any errors
A realist in time management and goal setting
Will follow directions precisely
Exemplify quality control and accuracy
Analyzer and thinker; like facts and logic
Like harmony and therefore dislike open confrontations with
  others
Dislike any form of carelessness or disorder
Do not like overly aggressive people
Neat and organized in dress, desk, home, and car
Can be critical and picky
Keen intuition plus worry may cause inner anxiety

If you are a salesperson:

Very good in planning territory and calls
Highly competitive, but with self rather than others
Ask nonthreatening but exacting questions
The most thorough of the four types
Very well prepared for every call
Good at analyzing prospects' problems
Excellent in selling highly technical goods and services
May dislike cold calls or pushing hard for a close
May be overly sensitive and take rejection personally

If you are on the buying side:

Highly analytical: you want specifics and track record
Dread making a mistake: overbuying, paying too much
Know how to ask the key questions
Uncanny knack of getting to the truth
Will uncover the lie or flaw in any sales presentation
Quite friendly, but the toughest to bring to a decision
Sensitive and intuitive; very careful in making a decision
Can't stand overly aggressive salespeople

PROBABLE TRAITS OF VARIOUS COMBINATIONS

People usually have more than one strong influence in the white area of the DESA GRAPH. Look for your own combination in the following examples. The highest on the DESA GRAPH would be the first word in the combination. For example, if the highest is ANALYTICAL with the next highest as SOLID, the example would show as ANALYTICAL/SOLID.

DOMINANT/EXPRESSIVE
Aggressive and competitive. Quick, and relentless in going after what he or she wants. Restless, task oriented. Wants to run things. Likes challenges. Weakness: may be too independent and insensitive to other's needs.

DOMINANT/EXPRESSIVE (EVEN)
Very ambitious and aggressive but can appear low-key. Likes prestige and influence. Uses charm and persuasion to obtain goals. Poised and very adaptable to conditions. Weakness: can be rebellious and also inconsiderate.

DOMINANT/SOLID/ANALYTICAL
Demanding of self and others. Self-reliant and goal oriented. Maintains very high work standards. Highly efficient and logical. Sees a job through. Weakness: instead of delegating may get impatient and do the task himself.

DOMINANT/ANALYTICAL
Here is a very perceptive, quick thinker. The analytical tempers the impulsiveness. A tough buyer. Aggressive. Domineering. Very creative in solving problems. Weakness: can be impatient, moody, bored, or "picky."

DOMINANT
Very self-reliant. A pioneer. Looks to new horizons to explore or exploit. Quite independent. A loner. Completely task oriented no matter what it takes. High ego. Weakness: can be opinionated, impatient, overly manipulative.

EXPRESSIVE
Dramatic, emotional. Likes spotlight, prestige, variety. Very social and outgoing. Quite optimistic. Abhors forms, financial reports. Likes one-on-one talk. Weakness: can be disorganized and has problem with time-management

EXPRESSIVE/ANALYTICAL
Competitive and goal oriented. Persuasive, charming, and articulate. Unlike the pure EXPRESSIVE, this person is usually organized. Desk neat. Weakness: may be too restless, sensitive, and impatient with friends and family.

EXPRESSIVE/DOMINANT
Ambitious, enthusiastic, confident. Disarms with spontaneous charm. Likes prestige. Although friendly, actually quite independent and restless. Weakness: poor time-management, may gloss over details or "wing it" with talk.

EXPRESSIVE/SOLID
Influential and dependable. Very warm and trusting. A loyal person who gives great support. People oriented. Excellent listener. Has great empathy. Resents "pushiness." Weakness: at times can be too lenient, too trusting.

SOLID/EXPRESSIVE
Great empathy. Personable, mature, logical, poised, dependable. Good team player. Influences with warmth, easygoing charm and sincerity. No pretenses. Honest. Good listener. Weakness: may sometimes be too "logical" or careful.

SOLID/DOMINANT/ANALYTICAL
Very self-reliant. Expects high performance of self and others. Sets high standards for others. Exacting. A "doer." Loyal, good team person. Patient (except with anything slipshod). Weakness: may not like to delegate.

SOLID/ANALYTICAL
Very self-organized person who pursues ambitious goals in systematized fashion. Analytical and unemotional in approach to problems. Independent. Deals with facts and logic. Weakness: can be too unyielding to others.

SOLID/EXPRESSIVE/ANALYTICAL/DOMINANT
Can be an overachiever. May be compulsive worker, even take work home. Self-reliant and charming, yet may feel a frustration in accomplishment. Possible weakness: may be too self-critical in trying to please others.

ANALYTICAL/EXPRESSIVE
Two things pull at this person: a need for lots of variety coupled with a systematized life. Goal oriented and quite charming. A planner. Neat and organized. Persuasive. Weakness: may be impatient, perhaps critical.

ANALYTICAL/SOLID (LOW D)
Mind like a steel trap. Very analytical and clear thinker. A perfectionist. Worries because intuitive sense points to what and who can go wrong. Quiet, systematic. Possible weakness: may be overly sensitive to what others think.

ANALYTICAL/SOLID
Competes with self rather than others in reaching goals and high performance. Likes exactness. Probably technically oriented. Similar to graph above. Somewhat cautious. Weakness: although very diplomatic can also be aloof.

ANALYTICAL/EXPRESSIVE/SOLID
Very confident of own abilities. Both a planner and performer. Has both logical and systematic thinking coupled with social and "people" enjoyment. Follows through. Weakness: although listens well, can be opinionated.

ANALYTICAL/DOMINANT
Very creataive in analyzing, solving problems, and planning. Independent, intuitive, demanding of others, and aggressive with own plans. At times moody, bored, or aloof. Weakness: can be picky and impatient with friends and family, or close associates.

CLUES TO PROBABLE BEHAVIOR STYLE

The following are some clues to help determine a person's probable behavior style. These are probabilities only. You may look down the list and notice one or two that do not fit your style. Keep in mind that most people are not "pure" types. They are usually combinations, as shown in the white area of the DESA GRAPH.

Here's an example in using some clues. A person might seem like an Expressive type; quite talkative, a good dresser. But you also notice the paperwork is neat, as well as the inside of the person's car. You would probably be dealing with an Expressive/Analytical combination. You would pay attention to factual data and precise planning, being careful to let the person talk and express his/her own ideas.

SOME QUESTIONS AND ANSWERS

Q: Can one's graph position change?

A: Yes, but gradually. A new responsibility can change one's style. However, if one horizontal bar on the DESA GRAPH is far higher than any of the others, then that style will probably be the predominant one for life. If two are close or almost even, then both styles would apply and either one could change.

Q: Which behavior styles get along best in working relationships?

A: The S seems to adapt and gets along best with all styles. Two D types may get along if they respect each other, but both will want their own way. An E and a D may at times have difficulty, as the D is task oriented and the "understanding" behavior of the E type might irritate the D. Two E types may have a lot of fun, but may not get much work done. A and D types actually work quite well together because each knows each needs the other. E and A types may have some problems since one is emotional, optimistic, and disorganized, the other factual and organized. Two A types get along and understand one another very well. The same is true, of course, with two S types. And the S and A types would have no problem.

Q: Which style makes the best salesperson?

A: There is no best style. It depends on the type of selling, whether it's high-tech, advertising, building long-range customers, the one-time sale, selling to stores, industries, or home buyers.

Buyers are far more sophisticated today. They demand creative problem solvers. Drive, enthusiasm, and warmth are still "musts," along with the ability to listen. However, the salesperson who understands the personality style of the prospective buyer has a great edge. The DESAnalysis provides this added tool.

Q: How accurate is the DESAnalysis?

A: The DESAnalysis is being used by corporations throughout the United States and Canada; by psychologists, salespeople, managers, trainers, and directors of human resources interested in building more effective teams within an organization. Accuracy feedback is running 80 to 90 percent.

SITUATION	D	E	S	A
ON PHONE	Friendly, but may be abrupt, authoritative.	Expressive, variation in voice, laughter.	Friendly, excellent listener. Possible monotone.	Noncommital in manner. Doesn't like any pushiness.
FACE TO FACE	Friendly, Sure of self. Quick. May interrupt. Direct. Intense.	Spontaneous and animated. Cheerful and friendly.	Warm, but quiet at first. Listens well. Opens up after he or she gets to know you.	Friendly, analyzing everything you say. Asks questions. May put you off—seeking more facts. Careful buyer.
INSIDE THE CAR	Could be disorderly. Too hurried to straighten things up. (unless there is S or A influence.)	Can be a mess; with all kinds of things on seat or floor.	Usually clean inside.	Very clean inside. Car well taken care of.
DESK	Many projects, too hurried to straighten things up. (Unless there is A influence.)	May be a mess unless someone is visiting. Then everything is jammed into already packed drawers.	Usually organized. Look for pictures of family on the desk, a name plate or things with name on it.	Usually very neat and well organized. Same with drawers.
BRIEFCASE	All sorts of materials, but may be out of order. (Unless A or S influence.)	Can be quite disorganized—particularly since this type collects things of interest from people and neglects to clear them out. (Unless A or S influence.)	Usually organized.	Well organized.
PAPER WORK	Hurried, brief. Large writing.	Can be hard to read, incomplete—or late.	Usually on time. If it's a report it will probably be an honest one.	Correct. Small printing or writing, usually. Very detailed if necessary.
MANNER	Intense, restless, quick, abrupt, confident.	Breezy, self-assured, good dresser. May wear latest thing out if E is strong. Trusting, optimistic, likes to talk. Likes variety and people.	Warm, easygoing manner. Confident, but conservative. Mature, poised. May smoke a pipe. High empathy but contemplative.	Precise. May show impatience with those close to them. Likes thoroughness in others.
LISTENING MANNER	Good for short periods then gets restless. Fidgets. May not hear you out. May interrupt.	May be looking right at you and nodding—and thinking of something else.	The best. Very compassionate listener.	Listens well—and easily. Catches the flaws.

7

The Magic of Charisma

*I*n human relationships nothing gets you to a goal faster than the magic of charisma.

Your charisma is how people feel about you. Your warm smile is picked up by the eyes of the other person and travels into the mind, where the emotions register a "liking" or "magical attraction" toward you. That person's brain lets you in, so to speak, to persuade and get the cooperation you want.

But a smile is only a part of the charismatic person. Charismatic people react to others in an alive, animated way. Much of their magnetism is the spontaneous interest in you and what you're doing. They make you feel important as they touch, nod, listen, look at you, and use your name. There is confidence in the movement of the eyes, face, and body. You feel their quiet strength of purpose in all that they are doing. They come across as generous and sincere. You can't help but like their delightful sense of humor and ability to laugh at themselves.

We are all being measured, evaluated, and pegged every day. Add just a little more charisma to your affairs with people and you will experience a whole new dimension in your influence. Add charisma to a banker, lawyer, doctor, architect, or engineer and you hear people rave about how great or smart they are.

Increasing charisma will get you where you want to go faster. It is truly magic in the way it opens the doors of opportunity. Yet, it costs us nothing. All we have to do is open our minds to it. Charisma really isn't very complicated. It is nothing more than the way you would want others to treat you.

Winston Churchill was a good example of the *desire* to become charismatic. In many ways he was a failure until age sixty. He was disliked in the House of Commons and had difficulty selling his ideas. Then he deliberately worked hard to develop his "people relationships." He methodically "programmed-in" the charismatic areas that were holding him back. Winston Churchill became one of the most charismatic leaders in history. Many of our great politicians, actors, and actresses have worked very hard developing what we see and feel as a very natural charisma.

You may be thinking, "What about shy people? How could they become magnetic, personable, and charismatic?" People who knew Albert Schweitzer say he was very charismatic. He exuded warmth, caring, and interest. The same is said of Albert Einstein. Yet, both were basically shy. They were not talkative, never the life of the party, but they did have a magnetic warmth that came through to people. One doesn't have to be in show business to have charisma.

What keeps a person from projecting more charisma is what researchers call "negative self-talk." Dr. Susan Glaser, professor at the University of Oregon, finds many people are prone to say all kinds of bad things to themselves. This self-deprecation and negative programming certainly isn't conducive to projecting charisma. What Dr. Glazer does is get them into a very relaxed state (similar to Deep Alpha in chapter 2) and help them see themselves acting and reacting positively.

We all express charisma. With some, it's a great deal; with many, it comes in little spurts . . . only when they feel like it. Some days it's more than others. Why not program into your mind some additional charisma that becomes a part of your everyday response? Below are twelve areas of charisma. Pick out one or two that you'd really like to improve upon. Each day, in Deep Alpha, repeat the suggested affirmations below that you like. They will gradually take hold as a Mind Set and become automatic.

Turn your back on this method to increase charisma and you are turning your back on keys to persuasion, increased income, fun, opportunities, job excitement, higher self-esteem, and wonderful personal relationships.

Some people couldn't care less about increasing their charisma. Basically, they do not like most people. They don't want to smile, or listen, or care about the feelings of others. Such people will now and then become charismatic in order to manipulate others. The warmth and concern is false, and it shows, unless they're exceptional actors. But even then, our intuition usually lets us know.

To increase charisma there must be the desire to care, love, and laugh with others, to listen and speak better, to feel optimistic, take risks, and welcome change. There must be the desire to be very open with others, and therefore, vulnerable.

THE TWELVE CHARISMATIC AFFIRMATIONS

1. "Today I Am Self-confident and Bold."

Charismatic example. John is physically expressive and sets the stage as he enters the prospect's office. It is obvious he has good feelings about himself. It comes across in his manner, walk, and appearance. He has a warm smile, maintains good pupil contact, and listens well. Nothing seems to rattle him. John knows what he wants and expects to get it. He agrees with Ralph Waldo Emerson: "Self trust is the first secret of success."

Opposite. Jake feels self-conscious when exchanging conversation with a group. He's inclined to look away when talking and listening. Jake slouches or finds something to lean on when talking to another. Also, he has some nervous habits such as twitching, scratching, putting fingers to his mouth or face, and fingering articles or clothing. He's inclined to be indecisive, timid, and anxious about many things.

2. "Today I Have a Good Rapport with Everyone I Meet."

Charismatic example. Barbara has an easy, warm manner that people like. As she goes through the day, she shows that she cares about people, paying attention to the things they say about themselves. Her very presence has a way of "lifting" people. She shares laughter and finds it easy to laugh at herself. Barbara *expects* to have a wonderful day as soon as she awakens in the morning.

Opposite. Nora does not like people and usually feels uncomfortable with strangers. The smile and greetings are put on. She does not trust people and looks for things to criticize in others. Nora resents any inconvenience brought on by another, such as a request for some information, a favor, or waiting. She is apt to be self-centered and sighs a lot.

3. "Today I Am Open and Spontaneous."

Charismatic example. Jerry is refreshing to be around. When he walks into a prospect's office he has zest and spontaneity. That doesn't mean he's loud. He simply cares about life and about the prospect and all the people in the prospect's office. And it shows. His honesty comes through as he openly expresses his feelings and emotions. He's quite relaxed, even a bit carefree.

Opposite. Parks is apt to be ponderous in giving a presentation. He's usually afraid to take chances and will frequently try to cover up mistakes or blame others. Parks is inhibited and tries not to show feelings and constantly worries about what people will think. He looks down much of the time and is overly concerned with self.

4. "Today I Am Strong and Decisive."

Charismatic example. Prospects and customers know exactly where they stand with Mary. She has a commitment to what she believes in and wants and is not afraid of being direct with anyone. Mary is totally self-assured, honest, tenacious, and tough, but with compassion. She does not feel guilty about having to say no. Prospects look to her for solid suggestions and help.

Opposite. Beatrice is overanxious, pessimistic, and indulges in self-pity. She is undependable, does not follow through, and will stretch the truth when necessary. She is "mealymouthed," indecisive, and probably wouldn't take a stand if there was opposition. She gives up easily. Beatrice smiles too much in trying hard to please.

5. "Today I Listen Intently to Everyone."

Charismatic example. Hank listens with his eyes and his ears. His rapt attention creates warmth and interest in others. His very attentiveness of leaning forward and responsive nodding is highly complimentary to his prospects. His own conversation and problem-solving are more intelligent because of his intense concentration on what the prospect has said.

Opposite. Ashleigh is not really interested in what other people have to say. He pretends to be listening while looking around or maybe nodding, but he is thinking of something else as the prospect is talking. He doesn't catch the real meanings in the voice inflections or changes in the eyes and gestures.

6. "Today I Help Build Self-esteem in Others."

Charismatic example. Marilyn is one of those wonderful "lifters" of people. In an office, people light up when she's around. Her very greeting says, "I like you, I think you are important." She gives the greatest gift there is, raising a person's self-esteem. She compliments people in front of others and is always enthusiastic about their goals and interests.

Opposite. Gertrude is indifferent to most people except the decision-maker. She frequently criticizes people in front of another or belittles a person's efforts. She's cynical, picky, and generally a very critical, negative person. In working with people, she can be quite inconsiderate, possibly overbearing, and sometimes condescending.

7. "Today I Remember Names Easily."

Charismatic example. When Jim made a new sales call he made it a point to get the receptionist's name, the secretary's name, and the names of any others at various desks in the office. When he got back to his car he'd write them down and make notations about their faces that would help him remember the names. On the callback a month later, he'd greet everyone by name as he passed their desks.

Opposite. Chad says he has a hard time remembering names. The truth is, he doesn't try because he doesn't care that much. Chad pretends he knows names with such phrases as, "How you doin', ol' buddy?" Chad doesn't realize how favorably he'd be remembered if he'd greet people by their names. He laughs off memory-peg techniques as unreliable. Chad needs to read chapter 9 in this book.

8. "Today I Am Positive in the Way I Talk, Act, and Think."

Charismatic example. Carol carries herself erect, and greets you with a warm smile, with her hand out. There's a lilt in her step and voice even when she's getting a turn-down. She enjoys life and people. Like anyone else, she has down moments, but she pulls back up quickly. You won't find her around negative people. Life's too short. Carol's successful manner and appearance attract the doers in life.

Opposite. Rhonda walks into a prospect's office in an apologetic manner. Because the prospect's business is off she really doesn't expect to sell anything. But it's good to keep in touch. She talks about others who have said business was bad, then drifts into some gossip and discusses personal problems, unaware that her prospect is starting to fidget.

9. "Today I Look, Act, and Feel Successful."

Charismatic example. Bill puts money into his clothes. He knows it's an investment . . . it's an investment that pays dividends. There's nothing "show-offy" about him, just a well-bred, clean appearance that shows a touch of class. It makes him feel more relaxed in making a presentation. The smart way he schedules his time shows in his purposeful manner.

Opposite. Horace cuts corners on what he spends for clothes. But he'll blow money on other things. He's a little careless about fingernails and scuffed shoes. He's apt to ramble in conversations, and his manner shows he doesn't have a good self-image. He worries a lot about things he can do nothing about. There's always junk in his car and he'd do better not to carry that tired briefcase.

10. "I Am One of the Best in My Business."

Charismatic example. People like experts. Laura's an expert in her field. She knows her business, the industry, and her prospect's business. Laura does her homework. She digs deeply into facts and figures and specific ways she can help the prospect. She's honest, professional, and extremely helpful with her customers. Laura has a high energy level, and plans her time well for maximum results.

Opposite. Maxine doesn't get much respect. She halfheartedly makes her calls hoping to pick up some business. She has some facts about what she sells, but doesn't know how to tie these into specific benefits for the prospect. So she wastes people's time in boring presentations. She takes an objection as a no answer and rarely makes callbacks.

11. "Today I Am Keenly Aware of What Each Person Wants."

Charismatic example. Tom is acutely aware of the feelings of the other person. He senses the emotional wants moment to moment. He knows when and how to be dramatic, when to talk, and when to shut up. Tom uses word pictures in making a presentation, and his concerned listening gives him the feedback to time the close properly. Tom follows his intuitive insights.

Opposite. Milner approaches every sales call the same way. He doesn't sense when a person is feeling pushed. He is insensitive to a prospect's obvious workload on the desk in front of him. Milner gets too close to the prospect or gets familiar at the wrong time. Milner is too self-centered to perceive the reactions and concerns of others.

12. "I Stay in Shape Physically and Mentally."

Charismatic example. Ann knows that charismatic people are healthy people. She looks and feels alive and enthusiastic. Her mind is alert with ideas in solving problems and showing prospects the benefits of what she sells. No overdrinking or overeating for her. She knows that anxiety brings on the temptation to overeat. Ann stays in shape with the right food and exercise.

Opposite. Nadine has to have extra cups of coffee to shake off a few too many drinks the night before. Somehow, she thinks she can bluff her way through with a sharp presentation. She overloads her stomach and feels sluggish. She spends too much time sitting, reshuffling papers until she can take off for home a bit early for a pick-me-up drink and an evening in front of the television.

The Rewards

Turn on your magic! Pick one or two of the above that especially appeal to you and program your mind with the affirmations. They will unfold gradually and become a part of you. You'll see it in other people's positive response toward you. You'll be building others' self-esteem along with your own.

8

The Pendulum Influence

*T*he vibrations between any two people are always in a state of change. Like the changing seasons and the ebb and flow of the tides, all personal relationships are in a constant flux. You feel these subtle changes with friends, with your spouse, with people at work. I call it the Pendulum Principle. In the art of persuasion it is vital to understand it and to make it work for you, not against you. In this chapter you will learn how to harness this force.

Think for a moment about someone you are with a great deal. You may feel close to that person one week and the following week the relationship seems a bit strained. Then it may level off for a while until some circumstance makes it change. In long-term relationships this ebb and flow may not have great peaks and valleys, but there is some change going on.

This flux is going on in all business relationships. However, most business people do not understand it as a constant phenomenon. Understanding these swings gives you great leverage over your competition. It is a little like the up-and-down values of the stock market. Conditions and the public's attitudes toward a certain stock affect its constant change.

Starting immediately, you will be aware of opportunities to take business away from the competition. At this moment, changes are going on between your competition and their customers. Their relationships are in an upswing or a downswing. They are getting better, or getting worse. That goes for each and every one of them, large and small accounts alike.

Let's look at relationships with your own customers for a moment. Consider that you are on a scale of 1 to 10 with each of your customers. That scale is changing slightly day to day. With one customer you might be a 7½ today and go to an 8 tomorrow following a nice lunch you had together. Two weeks later there is some problem. You were out of pocket and didn't get back to your customer until the following day. On your scale, that customer now emotionally feels less close to you. Let's say you are now a 6.

You are soon able to straighten things out, and before long you're back to an 8. Back and forth these feelings go. It can also work both ways. After a sarcastic comment from your customer, your emotional feelings toward him might drop to a 6.

You can make the Pendulum Principle work for you with customers, prospects, people at work, in all your relationships with others. Here are eight ways:

1. Flatten Out the Peak and Valley Attitude Gyrations

Keep that good rapport you have with customers by never taking their business for granted. Don't let even a little shift in attitude develop. As soon as you sense a slightly strained relationship, do something about it. Pay attention to your intuitive insights regarding their ego needs. Be open and aboveboard with them. Take care of that customer the way you did the first month you had the account. Stay alert to this ebb and flow of attitude toward you, keeping it on an even plane as much as possible. Be careful of any constant negative self-talk toward a customer. Your thoughts are *not* private. One way or another these feelings will be picked up by the customer.

The same principle applies to your superiors and others where you work. You keep the relationships on a high level by being concerned with their interests, their problems, and how you can make their job easier, in finding ways to help them look good to others.

You need also to "sell" within your own company, letting your people know how important they are to the customer or prospect relationship. When the people at your company know you care about them they will care more about you. Caring more about you affects the way they care about your customers. When your customers and prospects call on the phone they'll be greeted with warm recognition by others at your office. The lilt in the voice is a form of that recognition that shows your customer or prospect that everyone at your company really cares about him.

One thing about your long-term customers is that you do have at least some protection against losing them. That protection is the ignorance blinders your competitor is wearing. When you're in a downward swing with a customer of long standing your competitor is not likely to sense it. They assume your relationship is solid. Therefore, the sales calls they make on your customers are half-hearted presentations.

If you don't believe this, ask your good customers about the degree of expectancy and good selling by your competition. Many such calls are made just to comply with the request of their sales manager, or simply to "check it out."

2. Use the Pendulum Principle to Exploit the Competition

Use this principle to exploit your competitor's territory. You will find the "firmly entrenched" business, in many cases, is not firm at all. Be choosy. Go after the accounts you want. Do not be misled or "psyched out" by what appears on the surface. So the competitor plays golf with that account you want. That does not mean conditions are necessarily rosy. They may be deteriorating, or they may be getting better.

Go in with a warm, assumptive attitude—an inner attitude that you fully expect to be handling their business. This attitude becomes easier and easier as you form the daily habit of programming your mind. You must "sell" your subconscious mind that you have the account. To do that requires belief. You don't want to attempt to program your mind with something you don't really believe. That causes "kickback" and can be self-defeating.

It's better to program your mind that "you are finding ways to *help* this prospect." See yourself shaking hands with "Mr. Right" and the influencers. If you've already made a call on the prospect, review the mental images of the place in your mind. Millions of neuron connections are made in your brain each time you do this. If you can get some emotional caring about the company and the people you've met on previous calls, you'll intensify the connection procedure in your brain. Your very vibrations of such thoughts will reflect in your manner, in the feelings you "broadcast."

When you are on the way to a call at that company—or any company—make the affirmation that you and the prospect get along fine, that you will have a good rapport at the meeting. Do this several times *out loud* in the car as you're driving.

This kind of positive thinking reflects itself in your total manner. It is hard to resist. During in-depth interviews with corporate decision-makers, we were quite surprised how many expressed some resentment or dissatisfaction with their suppliers of long standing. Out of habit or because of inertia, they continued the relationships. What opportunities there are out there! How open these people would be to a good competitive presentation. And there's no stopping you if you will discipline yourself to use the tools of mind programming.

3. Go after the Accounts You Want

Go after the prime accounts, the large accounts. But be realistic. Can you honestly *help* those accounts? If those accounts are really better off with the competitor, then they should stay there. Your own company may not be set up to service the business properly, handle the production requirements, provide the necessary number of technicians, or whatever. And if you get the business by misrepresenting the facts, you will only weaken your self-confidence, plus, in one way or another, hurt yourself.

On the other hand, be alert to *hidden* opportunities of how you can help a prospect. Keep in mind that every service, every product, every company has some weak points. If your competitor is very large and dominates the market, this very bigness may be the cause of a lessening of personal concern with the customer. Also the customer may be getting service from newly trained employees, rather than service from an experienced person of a smaller company. If the prospect is a plum and the company appeals to you, it certainly deserves exploratory calls to get a "feel" of how you can help.

Let's get one thing straight about positive thinking. Simply meditating and visualizing yourself having large, new accounts is meaningless without active preparation. The active preparation is causing millions of new neuron connections, and the action is in itself a form of positive thinking. You see this with professional athletes and successful people who may not actually set a time for meditation, but they are meditating in their active preparation and the *high degree of the results they expect . . . and visualize.*

Learn all you can about the prospect before you make your first approach. Prepare well. Know that you're probably in for a series of callbacks. Decide, in advance, your contact pattern. In your kind of business how many calls, on the average, does it take to get an account?

Consider this fact: The average sale is wrapped up after the fifth call on a prospect. Let's look at the psychology of why this is so. It goes back to those connections in the brain. Each time you talk with someone on the phone or in person, more and more of these connections are made. The person's brain is impressed in a very physical and chemical way. On the first call we are strangers. Our senses are taking the other person in and relating the information to previous, similar information. Thus, a person may remind one of someone else. You note that the person bites his fingernails and that comes through regarding some previous information. You pick up some intuitive feelings about the person. Although millions of connections are being made, the pathways in the brain have not been established to a great degree. Now, let's say you like the person. You like the person's directness, smile, and warmth. Such an emotion causes much intensity in the connections.

A second call brings on a feeling of acquaintance. The feelings of the previous call are reinforced, millions of new connections are going on minute by minute during this call. We become somewhat of a friend/acquaintance on the third call, with further activity in the brain. But then, let's say something was said that the other person didn't like. There is a bit of a swing downward emotionally . . . all registered in the neuron network. But a fourth call reinforces the good feelings, and the swing goes up. This is supposing that your calls are short, not disruptive, and that you have something to offer on each call . . . a smile, listening interest, and something even slightly new over what you presented the previous times. Now, let's see what is actually happening to the *level of the relationship* as we go through a series of contacts.

4. Give Others a Chance to "Mesh Their Identity" with You

We tend to mesh our identity with others whom we like. If you have been interesting and warm on those callbacks, if you were knowledgeable and sincere, if the calls have been frequent enough, then the prospect's brain connections have provided a very definite pattern of likability and respect. You and the prospect, in a sense, have *meshed* your identities.

This can best be explained in the way that we mesh our identities with things we own. An example of this might be your suitcase. In an airport you watch for it as all the luggage parades around the beltway. Then you spot yours. You have a friendly feeling toward it. It's more than just yours—aside from someone else's—it is a part of you. That particular piece of luggage is well logged in your brain. The same with your car. It sits there among a hundred others in a parking lot. But as you approach it, you feel a kind of identity with it. There is a warmth toward it. It is the same with people in your life. A meshing of identity develops.

But let's take the example a step farther. Your luggage on the beltway looks shabby compared to the other luggage. You feel a little contempt for it, and it transfers into a trace of contempt for yourself. So it is with people. We don't want to identify with people for whom we have contempt. A winner doesn't want to identify with a loser.

In selling, we must plant the seeds of this "belonging" factor. The cultivation begins with a series of contacts properly spaced. Sincerity breeds trust. Benefits are pointed out, using as many senses as possible. Interest in the prospect, as a person, furthers the favorable neuron reinforcement.

Yet, how sad that the great majority of salespeople never cultivate this "belonging" factor. They don't fertilize, they don't water. Here are the facts: 80 percent of salespeople never get beyond the third call. The payoff is just a few calls away. But *80 percent quit too soon!*

Form your own call pattern depending on the economics and the geography you have to cover. In some cases it may be six phone calls, interspersed with mailing. Whatever way you choose, be sure that with every contact your attitude is one of high expectancy. You fully expect this prospect will soon be your customer. You are using the power of the assumptive close right from the beginning and through every callback and contact.

Here are more reasons to stay with your long-range call pattern: Consider the month-to-month changes in a corporation's forecasting, marketing strategy, financial position, sales thrust, goals, and problems. Consider the fact that a competitor may have switched a sales rep. The customer may not like the new sales rep, or the sales rep may lack experience. That customer might be very receptive to another seller.

It's so easy to assume . . . and not to make those calls.

5. Get More Business from Present Customers

Think a moment about your present customers. You've undoubt-edly been sensing those upswings in their attitudes toward you. The upswing is the time to go after an even larger piece of the customer's business. But first investigate. What other departments can use what you sell? What other divisions of the corporation might be able to use what you sell? What about increasing the quantity they buy? Are you selling them your full line? Every salesperson has favorite items or services they push. Favorites may be where there's the least resistance.

Here you have a prime prospect—your customer. Because your customer trusts you, the resistance level to your suggestions may be quite low. Of course, the mental preparation should be sound before pushing for additional business:

Think through the benefits to them.
Where will the budget come from?
Who would give final approval?
Who are the influencers?
Get some input from influencers before presenting the plan.
Put a simple plan on paper, outlining benefits.
Wait for the upswing in mood to present to the decision-maker.
Continue going after it. Simply watch your timing.

6. Use the Element of Surprise

In going after a large account, consider all the possible ideas you could use that would introduce an element of surprise . . . pleasant surprise. The competitor they are using may be in a rut, providing the same thing in the same old way. So brainstorm some ideas with others at your office. What interesting, bold bit of showmanship could you provide in the presentation? What new plan, new training service, new inventory stocking, new delivery plan or marketing service could you provide? Let your intuition work on this. In our interviews we found many decision-makers bored with the same old methods. They welcome sound, imaginative ideas. Remember, too, your new ideas can make the decision-maker look good to others. Most people do resist change; not so your entrepreneurial decision-makers. They are constantly changing things and looking for new ideas.

7. Boost the Level of Your People Relationships

Let's say your relationship level with a customer, your boss, or an acquaintance is fine. You sense that the ups and downs between you are minimal, with no real problems. How about taking the entire relationship level up a few pegs? It is done by getting on a more personal basis. To do this there must be real caring on your part. Nothing phony. It should only be done if you really want to. You, perhaps, become more open about your own life, even about your own weaknesses. In your self-talk you have a strong feeling of caring and respect for the other person. Call it camaraderie, depth of friendship, or whatever, it is a special liking toward that fellow human being.

Oh, I can hear some readers saying, "Hold on, you're just asking for trouble when you get too personal with people." Yes, there is definite risk. But the personal satisfaction, the fun, and other rewards overshadow the risk. The risk, of course, is that by boosting the entire level to a more personal plane you also have the possibility of sharper peaks and valleys. When there is caring there is also the possibility of hurt. Think for a moment what person or persons you would like to know better. These could be customers, acquaintances, or people at work. Begin any way you can think of to push that relationship up a few notches. It's up to you to make the move. You must take the lead.

You see, the great majority of people fear risk, fear rejection, fear being misunderstood. The great majority are not assertive, not aggressive; they will not take the initiative in pursuing and developing more meaningful relationships with others. So it is up to you. It could begin with anything from having them join you for lunch, or some event, or simply dropping by to have a cup of coffee with them.

8. Make Use of Maslow's Needs Hierarchy to Influence Relationships

A key cause of the ebb and flow swing in all relationships is a person's changing needs. You probably recall psychologist Abraham Maslow's hierarchy of needs from your college days. These start with the basic needs of food, water, sleep, and sex. In today's society these are usually met and therefore not a problem.

Now let's jump into Maslow's second set of needs. These are our safety and security needs. If you are called into the boss's office and criticized for something, there is an immediate downswing in your feelings toward the employer. This would be emphasized by your sudden need for security. Thoughts of looking for another job might cross your mind.

Suppose the next day the boss suggests you have lunch together. During lunch he asks if you would mind heading up a certain committee. After what had happened the day before, such a request might fill a longing need and be received with great delight. He would immediately be satisfying your third set of needs, that of belonging and love. You would feel an upswing in attitude toward him. He, in turn, might feel an upswing toward you since you could be satisfying a security need. He might be concerned about decisions the committee has been making and feel you would add a stabilizing influence.

However, if you were already on three committees, felt secure at the company, and felt support at home, his request might make little difference on any swing in your attitude. Your needs of belonging had already been met.

Instead of asking you to head up another committee, let's suppose he asks you to be on the program with him at the annual spring sales meeting at Hilton Head. He wants you to talk to the group about problems and solutions in managing national accounts. Now we are into Maslow's fourth set of needs: approval and esteem. The other needs have been met. Your basic physical needs have been taken care of, you feel secure, you feel you belong. The next set of needs is approval, recognition, and a healthy respect from others, plus additional self-respect. That's what the boss has provided. You feel the glow of an upswing.

The boss is also experiencing an upswing, but not from satisfying the same need. Let's say he's president of the corporation. He's secure, making plenty of money, has the feeling of belonging, and gets plenty of recognition. So what's left? The need for self-actualization. Maslow explains this as benevolent, brotherly feelings toward people, creativity, and enjoyment of interpersonal relationships with others.

He's bringing you along in the company. In a way he's playing the role of coach, and he's getting satisfaction not only from creating the conference format, but from giving you a new level of exposure.

In being sensitive to the ebb and flow of all relationships, keep the above five sets of needs in mind. Try to determine in your own mind where there is the greatest level of need in the other person. Find ways to help the other people fulfill that particular need, even in a small way. As you do that, you effect an upswing in their attitude toward you. Keep in mind, too, that a person's needs can shift from day to day . . . sometimes from hour to hour. I like to classify some of the sets of needs as "wants." We'll get into that in the chapter on "Motivating Others."

9

Your New Super Memory

You're introduced to another person. You look at each other, say hello, say your names. Nine seconds later the chances of recalling each other's name is down to 46 percent. At eighteen seconds the chances of recall have dropped to 23 percent.* However, by doing a few simple things, the name goes into the long-term memory, the figures are reversed, and there is high recall.

Most people have trouble remembering names. And most people treat it as a private, somewhat embarrassing problem. But no manual came with our beautiful memory machines. There were no simple instructions on how to get a name out of short-term memory into long-term memory. So we continue to use that friendly cover-up: "Hey, how's it going?" There's nothing wrong with that, but it doesn't fool anyone. How much nicer it would be to say, "Mary Thompson! I haven't seen you in a long time. How've you been?"

What a treat it would be for Mary Thompson to hear you speak her name. It's a compliment. It's a warm "lift." The ability to remember a person's name, to smoothly and clearly introduce that person to others, is one of the most powerful tools of persuasion and influence.

Being in sales, I was determined to find a simple answer to the problem. Some of the memory book methods were so cumbersome or complicated it hardly seemed worth the trouble. I wanted an easy method that really worked. What I came up with is based on

---

* This information was derived from studies of the retention curve of the short-term memory, conducted in 1981–1982 by Patton Communications, Inc., Houston, Texas.

the memory-peg association idea. I call it the LASAR system. It is spelled out in my book, *The Psychology of Closing Sales*.

I'm going to recap it here. With this system you will increase your memory recall of names fivefold in just twenty-four hours. And that's just part of building a super memory. In this chapter you will learn the following techniques that can be applied easily and quickly.

1. Recall names quickly.
2. Instantly recall a group of facts.
3. Remember key information from books or materials.
4. Remember the phone numbers of relatives and friends.
5. Remember a "to do" list.
6. Recall the influencing components of a presentation.

What We Know about Memory

Knowledge of how the memory works is rapidly unfolding. Scientists are discovering new methods to tap our great memory potential. It has been known for some time that there is a short-term memory, a temporary rehearsal buffer, and a long-term memory. But there was little to tell us how quickly to retrieve names and facts as we needed them. The techniques here are the keys to our new super memory. They are new methods of transferring information from the short-term memory to the long-term memory for future instant recall.

Apparently, memory is closely linked to the protein synthesis of the neurons and changes in the grids at the synaptic gaps. It is known that learning increases the RNA ribonucleic acid and protein synthesis. To maintain a sharp memory, it is critical to continue learning throughout life with an active interest in one's environment. Two other factors play an important part in maintaining a sharp memory. One is the motivation or desire to remember. The other one is high expectancy. You must *expect* to remember. This is so important in overcoming those years of bad conditioning. How often have we heard or said, "I can remember faces, but I can't remember names"?

Dr. Georgi Lasanov of Bulgaria has pioneered a new system of learning that just may revolutionize our teaching methods. It is a system of letting our minds become more receptive to information in an altered state such as Deep Alpha. Using a background of slow, classical music, information is repeated in rhythmic fashion. There are now courses based on this method in a number of universities throughout the United States and Canada. Proponents claim a five to fifty times increase of retention in learning new languages. We will be using some of these principles in retaining factual material.

How To Recall Names Quickly

LASAR is an acronym for a quick, five-step name recall. The first four steps would take place in three to six seconds after meeting a person.

1. *Look.* Really look at the person. Get some pupil contact.
2. *Absorb.* Listen to the name with high interest. You absorb it by giving some thought to it as you hear it. This is the most difficult part. Rather than concentrate on the other person's name, we may be visually distracted or think about the impression we are making on them.
3. *See.* You see a unique feature or a predominant feature on the face.
4. *Attach.* Mentally attach something visual to that unique feature of the face or hair. There are several ways to do this. Pick the one that works best for you. In your imagination, put an object in the person's hair. That object is the memory-peg association for the first name. The last name would be something "visual" hanging from a feature of the face.

For example, you have just met Jim Reynolds. For the first name, put a gym shoe in his hair. He has rather long blond hair, so string some of the hair through one of the eyelets of the shoe. Any such picturing strongly reinforces the neuron connections you are making in the brain. Also, those neuron connections will be reinforced with a broader network if you picture anything unique, emotional, or risqué. If Jim Reynolds has heavy eyebrows, "see" pieces of aluminum foil attached to his eyebrows. But let's say that Reynolds Aluminum means little to you as a memory association. Then you might use a person you know named Reynolds. See this person as a six-inch miniature hanging on one of Jim Reynolds's heavy eyebrows. You could also put a miniature person named Jim in the hair rather than the gym shoe.

Another way is to picture the gym shoe in the hair, but, instead of attaching something to a feature, think of the Reynolds you know as you intensely look at Jim Reynolds. When you use people instead of things use the first person who comes to mind when you think of the name. Here are two more examples:

You meet Joan Goldstein. Quickly you could put a six-inch Joan that you know dancing in the hair of Joan Goldstein, or you could use Joan Crawford. Then somewhere on Joan Goldstein's face you could visually hang a gold-plated stein.

You are introduced to John Gutirrez. You might visualize a miniature porcelain "john" in his hair. If the person had protruding eyes you might "see" some gooey stuff dripping out of one eye onto a miniature terrace right under the eye. The more bizarre, the stronger the neuron connections.

Here's a suggestion to keep the names locked in. Draw five to ten little faces on your prospect card or sheet. Label each with a name and approximate age. Then draw in what you saw, or what you attached. You don't have to be an artist. If there's a wart on the face show it on the drawing and print "wart" next to it. Do the same with bulging eyes, double chin, color of hair, and so on. Review your drawings from time to time. Notice the fantastic reaction when you make that callback two months later, walk through the office, and call everyone by name. Start this tomorrow!

Repeat. Use the name soon after you meet the person. Example: "What line of work are you in, Mr. Farnsworth?" Also, in the first ten seconds try to repeat the full name silently to yourself three times as you intensely look at the pupils and face. If you get a chance, write the name down. You will add strong neuron reinforcement through both the visual and motor activity by moving your hand to write.

How to Remember Facts and Key Information

When you're making a presentation and can drop in words and facts about the prospect's business you have gone a long way to outflank competition. You are a leap ahead when you can freely talk about the prospect's various products or services, know the names of various people in the branch offices, or intelligently discuss the demographics of their market share.

Suppose you're going to make a presentation to one hundred people. As you mingle with them before or after the meeting, it is a great help if you know their position and hometown. Or, suppose you are taking an exam and want to master the key points of the entire text. The following technique will lock it all in your mind for clear retrieval:

1. On your initial call gather as much information as possible in the form of brochures, organizational charts, house organs, and annual reports. Frequently, the receptionist or secretary can help on this. Don't hesitate to ask the person you're calling on. They will probably appreciate your interest. If you're going to make a presentation to a group, get the list of everyone who will be there, their positions, backgrounds, and where they're from.
2. Highlight or mark all key company points and key product and service facts. If you are going through a text, highlight or mark all the key points, chapter for chapter.
3. Get two or three cassettes of baroque music; Bach and Handel are excellent. You want classical music of about sixty beats to the minute.
4. Take yourself down to Deep Alpha and make the affirmation that you have a sharp and unlimited memory. State that you are going to program material into your memory and that it will all be clearly remembered.
5. In that very relaxed state open your eyes and turn on the music as background. In a steady rhythmic pace, read all those facts you have highlighted. Do not try hard. Just read out loud one sentence or fact after another. Read it through seven times.
6. Read it again twenty-four hours later. If possible, repeat a week later.

In *The Brain Book* (published in 1979 by E. P. Dutton, Inc.), psychologist Peter Russell outlines an excellent spaced repetition method: Review material ten minutes after you study it, again after twenty-four hours, one week later, one month later, and six months later. The method improves long-term memory retention from a 10 percent recall to an astounding 90 percent recall.

How to Remember a "To Do" List

Use twelve visual memory pegs. As you sit and think of things you must do, add the item to the memory peg. To start, you want to get the twelve pegs into the long-term memory. Do this by reading the following seven to fourteen times, so that when you think of any number there will be no hesitation. You will clearly "see" the object, or memory peg, for that number.

1. Bun
2. Shoe
3. Tree
4. Door
5. Hive
6. Pickax
7. Yen
8. Date
9. Sign
10. Hen
11. Pin
12. Elf
0. Deer

Now you're ready to use this to remember things you must do today. Let's say you must cash a check. Clearly visualize this between two halves of the bun. You need to call Hank, your printer. See a miniature printing press sticking out of the shoe. You need to call Rick Wilson about an appointment. Visually hang a big card with the name Rick on the tree. Carol's in the hospital, and you need to call and see how she is. See a hospital door. You need to see about that insurance claim on your car. See a bee coming out of a hive with a car bumper hanging on it.

That's how it's done. After making your list review it once to be sure you have them all in place. You may want to make the list according to priority. This little system will serve you well for the rest of your life. If you wish to expand it, just add more pegs. When possible make the pegs rhyme with the numbers.

How to Remember Phone Numbers

You now have a set of numbers with memory pegs in your long-term memory. Suppose you have a list of thirty phone numbers that you call rather frequently. Lock them into your memory bank for instant recall. Here's how:

Let's say your sister Jane lives in Denver. Her number is (303) 925–4532.

1. Start with the "nine" in her local number. Your memory peg for that number is "sign." Picture Jane holding a sign with one hand. At the top left hand corner is a twenty dollar bill and a five dollar

bill, held in place with a thumbtack. Painted on the left-hand portion of the sign is a World War II tank. The tank has the number forty-five on it, symbolizing the year the war ended. On the other side of the sign is a picture of your brother with a small blurb above his head that reads, "I'm thirty-two."

2. If an area code is involved, have the person holding a phone with one arm straight up in the air. That's your mental signal of the area code. On that telephone are three little pictures in a row. They should be connected in some unusual way. In the above, Jane would be holding the phone high in the air with her other arm. To recall area code 303, you need a picture of a tree, a deer, and another tree. In your mind you might see the deer stuck between the two trees. Try to make your pictures unusual.

3. Do no more than ten numbers at a time. You can do all ten at one sitting. On another day do ten more, and so on. As you build the pictures in your mind, get that person into the picture as much as possible. Notice how this was done above with Jane.

4. Make up the scene for each phone number. Then picture the scenes and recall the numbers seven times. If you miss any, continue a few more times. Twenty-four hours later go through them once, and then again one week later.

5. The scenes will be even more entrenched if you use the classical background music and describe the scenes aloud. First, get relaxed as explained above.

Making a Skillful Presentation

You can program into your subconscious mind the exact things you want to do in a presentation whether it's to one person or a large group. The following are suggested feelings and physical acts that you expect to happen:

We will like each other.
I will make good pupil contact.
I will feel very confident with this person (or group).
I will use silence effectively.
My small talk will be easy and warm.
I will ask good questions.
I will listen well.
Three key benefits that I will use are (*name them*) . . .

I am totally honest.
I will tie in the features (*name them*) to the benefits.
I will use visuals (*name them*).
The visuals will be very effective.
Everything will be presented smoothly.
I will use testimonial stories (*name them*).
I will handle objections with much empathy.
I will handle objections with a testimonial.
I will ask for the order.
I fully expect the order.
I am looking forward to working with this person or group.
If necessary, I will ask for the order again.
What I have will benefit the person (or group).
I will help that person (or group) enjoy those benefits.

Go into Deep Alpha as explained above. Open your eyes and read the list aloud in a rhythmic fashion to the slow background music. Go through it in a very relaxed way. Try seven times. Picture yourself feeling confident, getting pupil contact, handling the objection, reaching agreement.

Perhaps some of the things in this chapter seem like a lot of trouble. Don't pass judgment until you put these methods to the test. You will enjoy a new super memory. It will pay off and pay off in all your personal relationships for the rest of your life.

10

Screens and Influencers

*J*im Blake and I sat in his office talking about what *really* makes people want to buy your ideas. His company makes various packaging and packing materials for high-tech and general industry. I was there to help guide their selling to larger or more profitable accounts. Jim was a good salesman. He'd been selling for about five years, but he still had trouble getting in to see the right people. He explained how he frequently ended up talking with someone who actually didn't make the final decision. Supposedly, they would take his presentation to someone higher up.

"Jim," I said, "what you just said about *supposedly* taking your presentation to someone else is so right. Most of it stays right where you left it. You might as well have made a presentation to a wall. Actually, 64 percent of all sales calls are made to the wrong person."

"The screens?"

"Right."

"But what can you do about it?" he asked.

"Do it my way."

"You mean first call someone in the company to find out who really makes the decisions?"

"That's it. Believe me, Jim, if you'll use that method before you make any call on a new prospect, it will keep you from wasting time on the wrong people."

"That's okay, but see, the person I sell to is usually the purchasing agent. So that's who I try to make the appointment with."

"That's fine, but how do you know there isn't someone else at the company actually doing the recommending?"

"The influencers?"

"Correct. When a sale is made to a corporation the average number of influencers who are involved is now up to seven."

"Seven! Sometimes I have to get a recommendation from the plant superintendent and, occasionally, one of the vice-presidents, but I can't see where there'd be seven."

"Jim, every company is different politically. Titles on doors or on calling cards don't mean much. You have to get behind the scenes a bit to find out who influences whom.

"Let me give you some examples. Your warmth and empathy with a receptionist or secretary may influence her to give you some very needed information, or make the difference in getting to see her boss. Look, her boss can tell by the very inflection of her voice whether you're worth seeing or not. The boss depends a lot on a secretary because he or she certainly doesn't have time to see everyone. So, the secretary's got to be an efficient screen. And she may also be an influencer. Secretaries at the top management level frequently have plenty of clout. If she likes you she can put your call through to the boss, tell you the best times to see the boss or, possibly, set up a time for you, or directly influence the sale."

"Well sure, I'm nice to them, try to compliment them."

"It's more than being nice, Jim. It's caring . . . with real empathy. They're perceptive. They know if it's sincere."

"You mean 'flirting' is back in?"

"No . . . but, seriously, that brings to mind something I saw yesterday that was really dumb. A salesman came out of Rick Brown's office, stopped at his secretary's desk, mildly flirted a bit— you know, laughing and kidding. Rick came out and interrupted them by giving her some papers and instructions. His body language was all annoyance. Bosses are frequently possessive of their secretaries. They don't appreciate the familiarities of the "Don Juan" salesman. And, of course, women can't stand the "Greek god" type . . . the characters who are all wrapped up in themselves.

"Here are some other influencers that can kill or make the sale: the president, of course; the assistant to the president; an executive secretary; the comptroller or treasurer; a partner or part owner in the business. If you were selling directly to the consumer, like a real estate agent does, it would be a spouse; the kids; a close friend or relative; an attorney, or maybe an accountant. With you, Jim, it could also be: a design engineer; plant engineer; project engineer; head of production; purchasing agent or buyer; foreman; or a respected employee who would actually be working with packaging products."

"I can't get around to all those. Besides, if I did, and the purchasing agent found out, I'd be dead."

"Good point. I'm not talking about making an end run, Jim. I'm suggesting that on a new call you first find out exactly who the influencers are at each company, then start your contact as high as possible . . . with the final decision-maker."

"And work down?"

"Right."

"What about a prospect you're already calling on?"

"Unless you know you're talking to the decision-maker, you might say something like 'Miss Smith, if we get together on this, would there be anyone else sitting in on the final decision?' The key words there are *sitting in*. Those words aren't likely to ruffle the ego. If she tells you that Mr. Friedel would have to give a final okay on the budget, you might say something like, 'If it's all right with you . . . when we're finished here . . . I'd like to drop by his office on the way out . . . shake his hand, and tell him I'm working with you on this."

"What if she says she doesn't want you to."

"Don't do it. But Jim, most buyers won't object to that. Psychologically, you've made it very low key, with the casual handshaking idea. If you get an objection it may indicate the low self-esteem of the person you're talking with."

"What if you've made a number of calls over the past six months and you're getting nowhere? The person you've been dealing with indicates that he or she makes the decision, but you've got a pretty good feeling it's actually their boss."

"Do something different."

"Like what?"

"Like bringing in your boss to meet his or her boss, arranging a group presentation, which gives an excuse to have the boss and possibly other influencers present, meeting the boss socially, at a trade show or business conference, making contact when the screen is on vacation. And, of course, if you're not getting anywhere after a reasonable length of time, make the end run to someone higher up."

"Isn't that risky?"

"It is. But to be exceptional in anything you must take risks. This is simply a calculated risk; it's a judgment call. You haven't been able to get anywhere with your present strategy, so go to the top and try for it."

"All right, I'm going to take a shot at your method. I've got a prospect I need to call on, Palmer Industries. They sell a lot of graphic products to art stores and office supply stores all over the country. So, to get the political lay of the land, who do I call over there?"

"Call the sales manager. He could probably tell you who makes the final decision on buying packaging or packing materials, and he'd know who the influencers are."

"Suppose he's out?"

"Talk to someone in inside sales, head of accounting, secretary to the president or chairman of the board. They'll usually know. There's a sentence, Jim, that really gets cooperation from people."

"What's that?"

" 'I need your help.' "

" 'I need your help' . . . hmmm."

"Say it in a simple, warm, low-key way. Then explain the help that you want. You might ask who some of the people who would influence the decision are . . . what product they are now using . . . perhaps what they like about it or don't like about it. And, Jim, all it takes is a couple of minutes. Then you'll have a profile on the power structure before you ever go out there."

"Here goes . . . let me get their number."

"Jim, before you call them I've got a suggestion."

"Okay."

"Earlier, when you were making some cold calls trying to get an appointment you opened with: 'Ann Danberry? How are you today?' That's just waving a red flag that you're pitching something. It sounds so phony to someone you don't even know. The prospect's brain goes immediately into action to find a suitable negative excuse. Positive reception has been blocked out by past reactions to the awful telemarketing singsong pitches."

"I see what you mean. I've had some of those calls, and they're a pain."

"Now, let me pass on to you a technique that really motivates cooperation from the person you're talking with."

"What's that?"

"Smile."

"Oh, well, sure."

"No, Jim, I mean smile all the way through the phone conversation to the very end. It will absolutely double your appointment-getting. We've tested it and tracked it and that's the figure we get. I'm serious. What happens is that when you smile as you talk the shape of your mouth changes. This causes the sound in each word to have a bit of an upbeat lilt to it. This lilt comes across as warm and friendly, and causes an emotional warmth in the person you're talking with. It's simply an emotional response to cooperate with you."

"All right, stand by for smilin' Jim."

"Don't forget to use those responses we talked about if you get an 'I'm not interested' response on the phone."

Jim Blake got through to Arnold Crane, vice-president of sales and marketing. He explained that he needed Mr. Crane's help, that he planned to make a presentation to the company very soon, but he needed to know who would make the *final* decision in making any supplier changes in packing materials.

Mr. Crane was very helpful. After Jim got the final decision-maker's name he asked if there might be any others who could possibly influence the change. Crane probably admired his qualifying method. He came up with three names. One was very important: Tony Goss, superintendent on the packaging machines. According to Mr. Crane, this person's opinion was highly respected. He usually got what he asked for. This was vital information Jim probably would not have gotten from a receptionist or someone in public relations or the personnel department.

In this case it was a little difficult to determine the exact decision-maker. If the packing product was a new "concept" idea to these people, then Lew Taylor, the vice-president of production would probably be the final decision-maker. If Jim were simply trying to get them to change "brands," the final decision-maker would probably be in purchasing. But the information he got from the head of sales made him consider a different strategy. Because the superintendent, Tony Goss, carried so much weight the best tactic for either a "concept" sale or a "brand" sale was probably to get Tony's approval first. In a way he was the decision-maker. According to Mr. Crane, Tony got what he asked for.

It would be a mistake to call on purchasing first. Jim might put himself in a difficult position as far as ever meeting Tony Goss or the vice-president of production. He calculated that there was some risk by not going to purchasing first. But, as he had not met the purchasing agent, nobody would lose face. Because his packing materials might be considered a new concept the best bet was to first try to sell Tony Goss on the idea. What he hadn't expected was an immediate rebuff by Mr. Goss on the phone. Here's the way the phone conversation went:

"Tony Goss?" Jim remembered that you can usually get a warmer rapport immediately by using both names. It would be presumptuous to immediately call him by his first name, yet he didn't want to set too formal a tone by just using the last name.

"Yeah."

"This is Jim Blake with Ebberly Packaging Products."

"Yeah."

"We manufacture a unique packaging sleeve I'd like you to take a look at. If possible, I'd like to see you about ten after ten in the morning . . . or perhaps in the late afternoon around 3:45?" Jim was trying to smile as he said the words.

"Who'd you say you're with?"

"Ebberly . . . Ebberly Packaging Products."

"Man for you to see is Gary Clark in purchasing."

"As a matter of fact, I'm planning to see him . . . don't have an appointment with him yet, but I did want to see you just briefly while I'm out there. I've got an idea and I'd certainly like your input on it, something I want to show you. Is 10:10 okay, or would later in the afternoon be better?"

"Look, we're all fixed up on our packaging materials. Appreciate your calling, but I don't think we'd be interested at this time."

Jim handled this rebuff in the right way. "I can certainly understand that. It would be ridiculous for me to think I could call you this morning, and you'd say, 'Come on out, we want to change packaging suppliers.' Of course not, but I've got an idea . . . something I want to show you, that could possibly mean reducing shipping damage, but I need your opinion on it. So, if 10:10 would be okay, it would fit right in with my own schedule."

"Well, I'll be here. But I don't think we'll be making any changes."

"I understand. I'll see you at 10:10. My name, again, is Jim Blake."

"Okay."

"'Bye." Jim turned to me with a big smile. "Hey, that response to an 'I'm not interested' does work better!"

"You bet it does. Just tie it in with 'I've got an idea and I need your opinion on it.' Oh, those things don't work every time. Nothing does. But look at it this way: you've got to be a bit different. They don't have time to see every salesperson. So they're going to politely tell you they're not interested. You'd do the same thing. They get rid of about 95 percent of salespeople that way. A few salespeople try to hold them on the phone and push. But that only gets resentment. What you did psychologically was to show empathy, pique the curiosity a bit, completely relieve him of any obligation, plus one other thing."

"What's that?"

"You used odd times. In that man's mind he feels it will be a short sales call. You won't tie him up for a half hour or an hour. It helped influence him. Another thing, you didn't crawl or beg for a few minutes. In a professional way you got across that your time is valuable. You assumed some control by suggesting a time, rather than asking him when he could see you."

"You want to go out there with me on this call?"

"If you like, I'd be happy to. But you're going to do all the selling."

"If you're going to be an observer how should I introduce you."

"Be honest. Your company has hired me as a marketing consultant, and I'm just sitting in. That'll make it comfortable for everyone."

"Okay, I'll see you at about 9:30 then."

"Fine. By the way, what are you going to do now about preparation?"

"Like what?"

"Like names of competitors who sell to that type of business, the kind of packaging now being used for art supplies and drafting and office materials, maybe find out some complaints about present packaging, some likes and dislikes."

"I figured we'd pick up on all that when we get out there."

"We will . . . but what an impression if you knew some of it beforehand."

"What are you suggesting?"

"Making some personal calls this afternoon on three of the largest art and office supply dealers right here in town. Get with the managers and the people who unpack the shipments. You can be open with them. You're trying to get some background information at the dealer level . . . on complaints, what they like and don't like."

"Just walk in on them cold?"

"Why not? And use that sentence."

" 'I need your help'?"

"That's it."

Jim laughed. "Okay, I need your help tomorrow morning at 9:30."

11

Motivating Others

As we drove out to Palmer Industries, we talked about the influencing factors that are involved when a person decides to buy the idea you're selling.

"You know, this is an important call," Jim said after a few minutes of silence. I noticed his mouth had kind of a grim look.

"Feeling a little anxious about it?" I asked.

"Well, I found out they're one of the biggest suppliers in the business. And, of course, you'll be sitting there evaluating everything I say and do."

"I can wait in the car, Jim."

"No, no, I want your evaluation. I just don't want to do anything asinine."

"You won't. But don't ever be afraid to make mistakes. As the old saying goes, if you're not making any mistakes, you're not doing much."

"I guess that's right."

"Tell me, what do you really think of that idea I suggested yesterday to you and the others about programming your mind on the way to the call?"

"It seems silly saying out loud that you and the prospect are going to get along great."

"Have you ever tried it?"

"No, but that doesn't mean I don't believe in positive thinking."

"All right, Jim. You are now going to take the plunge of programming your mind on the way to a call. Let me hear you make the affirmation."

"Okay. Tony Goss and I will be real cozy, just like two bugs in a rug."

"Come on, Jim, make it serious."

"How about 'Tony Goss and I are going to have a warm rapport. We're going to get along great!' "

"Now do it again and add the words, 'I will find ways to help him.' "

"You're really sold on this stuff, aren't you?"

"It works, pal, it works. You're doing exactly what top athletes do when they psych themselves up. It comes across in the attitude. The other person picks it up in your vibes."

"This better make the guy real friendly. Okay, here goes."

"Let's hear it."

"Tony and I . . . we're going to get along great. . . . I'm going to find ways I can help him . . . help him and his company!"

"That's good. Now, do you feel anything different? I'm serious."

"Not really. Maybe a little more comfortable about the meeting."

"That's the feeling you want. And that brain of yours is already subconsciously sorting through ways you can help him. That's the key to selling. It's helping, helping the person get what he emotionally wants."

"What about what he logically wants?"

"First of all there's a big difference between a want and a need. You may logically need a very simple car. But emotionally you want a fancy sports car. So that's what you're driving. Almost everything we do, almost everything we buy is based on emotion. Logic is simply the mask we wear to cover the emotional desire. We like to be able to justify all our decisions, not just to others but to ourselves."

"How do you mean?" Jim asked.

"All right, yesterday I told you I really liked my soft contact lenses, that getting rid of glasses gives me more vision on the tennis court. That was my logic to you and to myself. *Emotionally*, I feel they make me look younger. That's the *real* reason for putting up with all that cleaning and soaking ritual. Vanity dies hard, my friend."

"I'll buy that. But what emotional reason would a person have to buy my packaging products?"

"Jim, there are four areas where an individual is most vulnerable to influence and persuasion."

"And they are . . . ?"

"Vanity, fear, presumed gratification, and self-approval."

"What about the profit motive?"

"That could be vanity."

"Vanity . . . how?"

"Power, status, recognition by others as being something or somebody. Those are strong motivational forces, Jim. And just because I lump a lot of feelings under the vanity area doesn't mean they're bad."

"But they could be."

"Sure, if vanity puts you into a Mercedes you can't afford, or your lust for making money is so intense it blinds you to the beauties of life, or if self-interest in front of the mirror or recognition by others is so all-consuming, there's no room for warm, caring relationships. Then, my friend, the cards of misery are stacked against you."

"Then one of the vanities of this man, Tony Goss, would probably be that he wants others to think he's important."

"Absolutely. I suppose we all do."

"Then, just because I want to feel important . . . I'm vain?"

"Now, Jim, you're overlapping into self-approval. Wanting others to think you're important could be vanity, and wanting yourself to feel important is liking yourself more, or self-approval. Much of what motivates us is a blend of various areas. Suppose, for example, you decided to get an M.B.A. degree. That could be vanity or recognition if what others would think gave you kind of a glow. It could also make you like yourself better . . . self-approval. Fear could be part of the motivation. You might fear you couldn't get ahead without the degree. Then presumed gratification would probably blend in as a motivator. You might presume enjoyment of putting the certificate on the wall, which, of course, would also be a blend of vanity. We humans are a load of many vanities, Jim, but if you don't like the word vanity, change it to recognition."

"No, I see what you mean."

"Without having met Tony Goss we can assume certain vanities. He probably eats up the approval he gets from his boss, the vice-president of production. He probably wants his employees to think he's a tough but fair leader. No doubt he wants his friends to think he has an important job. We can also assume he wants self-approval. He wants to feel he's smart, probably wants to feel he has good heritage, that he appeals to women."

"All right, what about his fears?"

"Many psychologists believe fear is our strongest motivator. Tony would fear disapproval by his boss, fear of being replaced by someone, loss of power. He might fear loss of respect from his employees, fear of any changes in the company, fear of being old, sickly, not having enough money, fear of losing someone's love. There are others, more specific, that we'll probably pick up on as we talk with him."

"Any presumed gratifications?"

"That's harder to pin down without meeting him. It could be a presumed gratification of a favorite food, a hobby such as fishing, getting to work before the others come in, keeping all his machines very clean, a fettish about neatness, a certain program on television. Much of the enjoyment in the presumed gratification is actually the anticipation, like getting ready for a date or ordering a chocolate fudge sundae. When people are bored, frustrated, unhappy, worried, or feel guilty, they can frequently be motivated into presumed gratification as escapes. In selling, it's so important to paint word pictures so well that people feel the presumed gratification as being very real. And, again, it's frequently a blend with another motivator. For example, getting a certain hairstyle might make a person look younger, so they'd like themselves better and enjoy comments from others, and the presumed gratification might be in how it would affect others' attentions.

"Another interesting example is the ski resort. A travel agent would show you a very colorful brochure. As you look at the pictures of happy groups on the slopes and sipping hot rum in front of the fire, you get presumed gratification of the enjoyment you'll have. There's presumed gratification in how you'll look in ski clothes and whom you might meet. If the travel agent gets you a special discount, you'll feel you made a smart buy; that's self-approval. You'll get in good physical shape; more self-approval. You can tell your friends about the trip: vanity. But the ad people who wrote the brochure were smart enough to know that the emotion of fear could kill your decision. You might have a hidden fear of looking stupid trying to ski, or possibly breaking your leg. So there are pictures of groups lounging around the pool with snow in the background, and fascinating places you can shop. Ah, your mind is relieved that it may be a ski resort, but you don't have to ski, and, of course, you saw the picture of the instructor with a beginners' group in case you do want to ski."

"Hmm, I was just thinking . . . "

"What?"

"As you were going through those examples, I was just imagining which motivating factors would apply to my selling Tony Goss our packing materials."

"You're right on track! What'd you come up with?"

"Under vanities, he would like us to feel he is smart, efficient, and a key person in their production operation. He might even want us to think he is tough. If he bought my product, he might look smart to his boss and his employees. In fact, if my product produced a noticeable decrease in shipping damage, it might get the attention of higher-ups. And such pluses don't hurt if he's bucking for the vice-president of production. Maybe that's stretching it."

"No, no . . . you're running out the string very well. And what about fears?"

"He might fear that if he changed to our product, it wouldn't work as well as what he's using now."

"Which would mean . . . ?"

"Which would mean it would cost his company money, loss of face and respect of the purchasing agent, vice-president of production . . . and, possibly, the employees working on the machines."

"Anything else?"

"He would lose some of his own self-approval, feel like a fool."

"Jim, there's a possibility of something else."

"What's that?"

"Fear of losing a pleasant relationship with some sales rep he's now dealing with or, simply, the fear of having to tell his present supplier he's made a change. That may not be a big fear, but it's frequently there. In our surveys we found that lots of people are not happy with certain business relationships but continue out of habit or dislike of confronting them about a change."

"You know, I never thought of that as an objection."

"It's a hidden objection . . . rarely out in the open. That's what makes it so tough. The spoken objections are used to hide it."

"Okay, I haven't even talked to this guy, and already we've got him completely unsold on using my packing products."

"You're doing fine."

"Let's see, to offset those fears I'd better name other companies that are using my product."

"Go a step farther, Jim. Give him some real anecdotes . . . some short stories. Make them come alive."

"How do you mean?"

"Real testimonials in the form of a plot. A certain respected company didn't want to buy your product; costs too much, happy with present product, or whatever. After a number of callbacks they tried it. Now they're happy, use yours exclusively. And in the story explain the benefits they like. Got some like that?"

"Sure."

"Jim, the anecdote is one of the most potent tools in getting credibility, handling objections, and getting a commitment. Yet, in our studies, 94 percent of salespeople do not use the short testimonial anecdote. They simply recite names of customers. It doesn't have the same influencing impact. The beauty is that you can move from the testimonial anecdote right into the close."

"Right into asking for the order?"

"Not yet. First, you go through how happy the customer you just mentioned is. Second, you say why the customer is happy. Third, you mention that you can do the same for them. Fourth, you paint very vivid word pictures of the prospect happy with your packaging product. You let him know that when he sits down with his people and compares his few returned damaged shipments of the last sixty days using your product, with the large number of returned damaged shipments of the previous sixty days, he's going to be very pleasantly surprised. That is painting the picture of presumed gratification. Of course, Jim, I'm assuming that this would be true."

"Oh, it's better than most of the competition. But a lot of them really clobber us on price."

"Jim, every product or service in the marketplace has a weakness. One company might have packing that doesn't take heavy abuse on the corners of the package. Your strength is that packages can withstand abuse, particularly on the corners. Your weakness is your higher price. Take the quality out of your product and you could come down in price. Then you'd have a strength in price and a weakness in product."

"So I must justify higher costs in packing against savings of less damage."

"Exactly, but not just logically; get emotion into it with word pictures."

"Getting back to that anecdote thing, I've got two good ones I could use."

"That's fine for today. But you should have at least six . . . preferably ten. The more you have, the better you can draw on them to fit a particular situation. Tonight, take those you have and say them in front of a mirror seven times. That way they lock in. You won't stumble and stammer as you go through it with a prospect."

"Use a mirror, huh? My wife will think I'm a narcissist or going nuts."

"Probably."

"Well, we're about there."

"Hey, Jim, I meant to ask you. Did you see any dealers yesterday to get a little better insight from them?"

"You better believe it. It was a good idea. There were some complaints about the art board packaging and also, sometimes, the briefcases get scratched up on the corners."

"Your prospect manufactures both briefcases and art boards?"

"No, that's another thing your idea helped me out on. I found out that Palmer Industries is actually a distributor for some items like briefcases, drafting materials, and some office supplies, and they manufacture a number of other items. So some of it is shipped out in the original cartons from another manufacturer."

"I'm reading your mind, Jim."

"Right, I've got leads on two other manufacturers not far from here. I looked at some of the packages; not too good. One guy was real upset. Said he usually unpacked out near his displays and that white, popcornlike packing would go all over the floor."

We turned on Wallisville Road, went about half a mile, and there was Palmer Industries. The front was a long, one-story building with a modernistic stone-and-glass entrance. From what we could see, it looked like a steel two-story in the back. That was probably the warehouse. We walked into the lobby.

I sat down while Jim introduced himself to the receptionist and signed the guest register. He checked through several pages of the register to see if any of his competitors had signed in recently. I liked the fact that he was quite open about it and asked the receptionist's permission first. This got him into a conversation, and he found that Emerald Packaging was their main supplier.

"They're tough," he sighed, taking a chair next to me.

"Who's tough?"

"Emerald Packaging. That's who has the business here. They usually come in pretty low on price."

"How about the product or the service? Good as yours?"

"Product's okay, except they don't have the sleeve we've got with the extra protection in the corners. So I'm going to have to build my case around that."

"And the service?"

"Okay, I guess. Haven't heard any complaints. One thing about Emerald, they do a good advertising job. Their packing bubbles are shaped like emeralds. So they push the theme 'Be sure your package is packed in Emeralds.' "

"Very clever. But don't let it psych you out."

"No, no."

"Does Goss know you're here?"

"Yeah. He'll be tied up for about ten minutes."

"Does the receptionist have any brochures, annual reports, house organs, or organizational charts she can give you?"

"Got me. Do they usually have that kind of stuff?"

"Frequently. It gives you input while you're waiting. Also, you'll want to read through it before you make your first callback."

"So you don't think I can sell him today, huh? Such confidence you have in me."

"I'm not worried about you. Anyone who flips through the guest register isn't afraid to ask for the order."

"Ah, you noticed. Did you also notice I asked permission?"

"I noticed. Hey, Jim, check that salesman who just walked in."

"You mean the one who's standing there with the fellow in the white shirt?"

"Yup . . . and he just made a big mistake."

"How?"

"The fellow in the white shirt came out here to the lobby and got the salesman to make a stand-up presentation to him. It's an old trick. Saves the prospect from getting tied up. They can get rid of a salesman in about three minutes that way."

"That happens to me sometimes, but what can you do about it?"

"Don't make the presentation. You can't win."

"But what do you say?"

"In a warm but firm way you let them know you have something to show them and ask if there isn't someplace the two of you could sit down for a few minutes. As you ask, take a slight step toward the door or hall the prospect just came through. It shows you assume he will do what you suggest. It works."

Jim got some product folders and other material from the receptionist and read them as we waited. Then he pointed to something in the annual report.

"Well, I'll be darned!"

"What?"

"This company is owned by Calgary Corporation. We sell a lot of product to them! That could be a real plus."

"Maybe."

"What do you mean *maybe*?"

"Sometimes what parent companies do is resented. So feel your way on that one. Don't make that your key point going in. Sell the benefits of your product first. Then, as an aside, let him know you sell to the parent company. Watch his eyes as you do this. If it's a plus, you'll see some satisfied relief in his face. You have lessened his feeling of risk in making the change. On the other hand, it may be met with indifference in the face and eyes. Then, obviously, don't press the point. Mergers and buy outs sometimes leave a bitter aftertaste."

The receptionist interrupted Jim's reading. "Mr. Blake, Mr. Goss said it would be just a few more minutes."

"Thank you, and thank you for this material. May I keep it?"

"Sure, I have plenty." She smiled.

"Jim, you were asking on the way out here about the profit motive, and I put profit motive, approval, and recognition all under vanity appeals. Many salespeople use the profit motive on the wrong people. Take most employees; they're not all that consumed by how much something will save or profit the corporation they work for. Their concern for costs is primarily related to how much *recognition* they will get for a *decision* that will save or make the company money.

"I've had people take exception with me on that one. They'll explain that they're more careful about the company's money than their own. That is frequently true, but the motive may actually be recognition that they're doing a good job."

"So, recognition and approval are the motivators for an employee, and even middle managers?"

"Usually. Then, at the top level, it's all bottom line . . . how much profit will it make, or how much will it save.

"Of course, Jim, recognition from the outside is different. Top management is always interested in something that would get good recognition from the media, the public, the industry, and the competition. However, that, too, could be the profit motive resulting from recognition."

"I get the feeling you think I'm overly concerned with the fact that I can't meet Emerald's low prices."

"Only as far as Tony Goss is concerned. But then, you won't really know until you get in there. Now, when you get to the purchasing agent after seeing Tony Goss, you may run smack into price. Although he probably isn't moved by the profit motive, he may pride himself on being a shrewd and tough buyer and enjoy that recognition."

"What do you do when a prospect just doesn't act too interested?"

"Rick Wilcoxon, an excellent sales trainer in Houston, talks about five negative attitudes of buyers. Number one is indifference. Number two is rejection, three is skepticism, four, procrastination, and five is fear.

"I like to think of these as roadblocks. You're going to run into at least one of these in every selling attempt. It'll be interesting to see which one you'll run into with Tony Goss. Let's take them one by one.

"A little while ago, Jim, you were talking about indifference. Consider the fact that purchasing agents may see ten to twenty salespeople a day. In most cases the competitive advantages aren't all that different. There's nothing there that really turns them on. Your job is to try to change that. In our interviews 88 percent of purchasing agents said to please tell salespeople to get some showmanship into their presentations. For example, on a sales call you might carry in some kind of heavy package. Then, somewhere in the presentation, you could drop it on one of the corners to illustrate your Corner Cluster Safety Sleeve. It makes it interesting, and you're remembered, while hundreds of other salespeople are long forgotten. Jim, always use some kind of visual on every call . . . the more dramatic, the better."

"I usually use our samples. I think they're good."

"I agree. What you've got there should get attention. Would you believe the average attention span of an adult is between one and eight seconds? If you don't believe it, try thinking of some object without any other thoughts coming into your mind. It isn't easy. Our thoughts are always flitting around our minds.

"Another thing about indifference. It's wiped out when the other person feels lifted by your presence, your warmth, your caring, or, perhaps, a sincere compliment or acknowledgment of their worth. Now you've got the motivation of both self-approval and vanity. If your word pictures trigger a presumed gratification in their mind, you probably have a sale."

"Let's see," Jim said, "number two is rejection. I guess they just don't like what you're selling."

"That, or they may not like you. Your vibes don't mesh. As a general rule, the more alike you are with the other person in background, interests, dress, and so on, the easier it is. Subtle prejudices come into play here. That could be speech, age, sex, race, even such things as a beard, shoes with tassels, certain kinds of jewelry, expression on the face, something about your appearance or manner.

"You could get rejection simply because a person can't afford it, doesn't want it, doesn't like it. Also, the person could have a load of other concerns. Your timing might be bad through no fault of your own.

"Jim, this might sound crazy, but if I'm getting rejection from someone, I ask why. It can be done in a very light manner. You simply stop talking and say something to the effect that you get the feeling that the person isn't really interested. Then you ask if it is you, or the presentation, or, perhaps, you caught them at a bad time. But, when you say something like that be sure you do it in a low-key, smiling manner. It works. It can turn a rejection right into a close."

"And number three, skepticism?"

"Skepticism is normal. The best way around it is proof. That could be anything in print. Psychologically, we tend to believe something that is printed. Use the anecdote, the short testimonial story we talked about. Better still, use them both in a presentation. And be careful you haven't gotten carried away with some exaggeration. Those are educated buyers out there."

"Okay, what about procrastination? I run into that a lot."

"The desire may be weak. Possibly you didn't target the strongest motivational area. The benefits aren't strong enough to get in a hurry. The presumed gratification isn't there. Possibly other things are more important."

"So what do you do?"

"Make regular return calls with slightly new approaches. Stay in touch by phone; also drop any articles of interest off to them. Use the anecdote of some other customer who was going to put it off but didn't. Tell why that customer is happy . . . how they avoided loss by going ahead. Use some special hooker method to get action. For example, all customers who place an order this month receive a certain premium.

"And do this: As best you can, mentally assume they are going to buy, ask for the order. You fully expect that they are going to make a decision to buy right now. The vibrations of that attitude come through. Keep yourself programmed with that assumptive attitude, painting strong pictures of what the person will soon be receiving. It's not all that easy to keep that expectant attitude, but it certainly gets results."

"And what about fear?"

"Jim, try to draw them out with questions to see if you can find where the fear is. If they talk long enough you'll usually catch it. It may be between the lines of what they actually say. Your intuition will help you here. And, of course, use those anecdotes . . ."

"Uh . . . I just may get the chance in a few minutes. I think this is our man coming."

12

Getting a Commitment

The man coming toward us had a large, square jaw and heavy eyebrows. He looked like someone who could take care of himself and probably anyone else.

"Which one's Jim Blake?" He half smiled.

"I am." Jim stood up, shook hands, and then introduced me.

Tony Goss's manner was very direct, almost abrupt. "What's this thing you wanted to show me?"

"I've got it right here," Jim said. "Someplace where we can sit down?"

"Yeah, come on in."

I knew Jim would have liked to look at me at that moment and say, "See, I didn't get trapped in the lobby."

We walked through some swinging doors past some tables of binders and stamping machines. Tony's office had a large window giving a good view of the work area. We settled down into chairs as Tony took his place behind the desk. The office was efficient, except for a heap of reports on the desk and some machine drawings on the floor in the corner.

Tony opened with "We've had a time today. One of our punch presses is down so we've had to make do with an older one we occasionally use. But it's been slow."

"What kind is the one that's down?" Jim asked.

"Well, actually, it's in the controls," Tony answered.

"You mean the NC system?"

"Yeah, we're not getting the right feed on the tape."

Tony suddenly seemed more interested. Jim was doing a good job with the small talk, letting him know he had a little more knowledge than what was on his price sheet for packing materials.

"What about your packaging machines . . . how are they controlled?"

"Manually."

"Mr. Goss, I was talking with Arnold Crane . . . and he certainly had some complimentary things to say about you. That's why we wanted especially to meet with you today. I'd like your input on an idea that just might be very helpful in your packaging . . . but, first, let me ask you . . . "

Jim, asked a number of questions about their packaging and packing methods. He didn't want to present his idea until he had some input. I thought he used the "pass along compliment" about Arnold Crane very well. It caused a bit of a gleam in Tony's eyes. However, when he got into questions about damaged returns due to packaging, Tony didn't give him specific answers. Also, Tony wiggled a bit in the chair, his eyes looked away, and he started scratching the side of his mouth. The body language showed that Jim had hit on something that bothered Tony. Ah, they *were* having some trouble with damaged returns.

Jim caught the body language and moved right in. But he was careful not to put his prospect on the defensive by being too absolute. He talked about some of the packaging complaints he got from dealers in general; how they liked the protection of Ebberly's "Korner Kushion Sleeve." Then Tony's lips pursed a bit; there was something that Jim said that bothered Tony. Jim didn't catch it at first. He showed how easily the corner sleeves are inserted and described how the special "tear bubbles" provide the cushion.

I now knew Jim felt something was wrong. He was expecting some good reaction when he showed the dramatic "before and after" pictures of heavy packages dropped on corners from various heights. Tony had a slight scowl. Jim tried a new tack to get Tony involved, or at least draw him out.

"Mr. Goss," Jim asked, "I'd certainly like to see some of your machines out there . . . is there a chance of getting a quick walk through?"

"Sure, come on. Like I said, we've got one of them down right now."

We walked past packages coming down a line of steel rollers and being loaded onto a dolly. Several people at the other end were putting disassembled easels into long boxes. Next to them, others were loading art boards. Tony stopped and we watched for about a minute. Jim recognized one of the packers as the same one pictured in the in-house publication he saw in the lobby.

"Believe I saw this man in a photo in your company bulletin," Jim said.

"You see, Mark, you're getting famous," Tony kidded.

Mark beamed a big smile. It seemed to break the ice for the first time. Tony turned to both of us, hesitated, then looked at Jim.

"You see, Jim, how they're packing those boards. They're pretty well protected. I'm not saying your corner sleeves wouldn't reduce damage, but we had an efficiency team go through the plant six months ago. We rearranged everything. It was a mess for a while, but on each station they found ways to cut time and movement. We've got this one down to a fast flow; the box, the boards, the packing, and a quick shot through the binding machine. Putting those sleeves in each corner would take that much more time in added motions. And that's something Lew Taylor doesn't want. He's head of production. Those guys who were here really streamlined it. I'll admit that at first I thought it was a lot of nonsense, but it's really cut production costs."

"That's great," Jim nodded.

"So you see what I mean by adding any costs."

"I couldn't agree with you more," Jim said. "May I call you Tony?"

"Yeah, sure."

"Tony . . . what you've done is cut costs. But the efficiency people had no way of knowing about damaged goods. They were interested in time and motion studies. Okay . . . now I need your feelings on this. Is it just possible that adding the sleeves, which would add some cost, might, however, actually cut bottom line costs simply by cutting way down on returned, damaged products?"

"Sure, it's possible. But we're talking about some unknowns. We really don't know what it would add to the motion cost. And we certainly don't really know how much damage it would stop."

"True, and, as I said, I just wanted your feelings on it."

As I listened to the two of them talk, I realized why Tony had pursed his lips in his office. He saw added time and motion on his production line. And that would go counter to what his boss wanted. He obviously admired his boss. When he spoke his name there was an upbeat in the way he said it. It's amazing how you can tell how a person feels about someone just by listening carefully to the inflection when they say the person's name.

Jim did a good job in establishing some rapport; he got on a first-name basis in a way that couldn't offend. Also, in a very steady way he was moving in on the close with Tony Goss. Timing is so critical in closing. How stupid it would have been to push for the close in Tony's office. As things looked, he would probably have to sell Tony, then Lew Taylor, and, finally, Gary Clark in purchasing.

At this point Jim was moving to the third stage in creating desire for his product. First, he got Tony to agree that there was a damage problem. Second, he let Tony know that possibly the corner cushion idea could help solve it. The third step was to somehow, right now, involve Tony with a mental image of "presumed gratification." Fourth, he had to turn that desire to positive action from Tony.

I saw Jim unfold one of his Korner Kushion Sleeves. Now I knew why he had carried it with him out of Tony's office. He was going to use some kind of showmanship to involve Tony emotionally.

"Tony, I want to show you something," Jim said. "Take your fist and put it in this Korner Kushion Sleeve . . . okay. Now, take your other hand, form it into a fist, and push against your fist with the Korner Kushion on it. Notice the cushion you get . . . like a mini shock absorber. Imagine one of those on each corner of that pack of boards as it goes into the box. Now, in shipping, that box is going to go through all kinds of shock treatment by people who just don't care. As I see it, with Korner Kushions in that box those boards are going to be unpacked in a store just as pretty as they are right here. By putting these Korner Kushions in each box I believe you would save Palmer Industries a great deal of money, and further Mr. Taylor's fight to cut production costs."

"Jim, I have no doubt it would cut damage . . . at least at the corners. But, as I said, we don't really know how much. We don't know that it would actually save us money, considering the materials and the added time to put them on the corners."

"I agree, and you're not alone."

Ah, Jim was now going to use a testimonial anecdote. "Tony, B. C. Armstrong in Chicago felt the same way as you. They ship a lot of VCRs and sound systems. They had their production and packaging well organized, but there was a regular flow of damaged returns directly due to corner stress and impact. Dick Saunders there pushed to run a test and track the returns of their regular package and the ones with the Korner Kushions. They told me that using Korner Kushions cut the damaged returns more than 65 percent. I feel we might very well do the same for you. We don't know. But if you run a test, and it works, you and Lew Taylor may be sitting down together sixty days from now and project a nice savings for the year by using Ebberly Korner Kushions."

"Yeah, we are getting returns on those boards that I don't like to see."

Jim knew a closing statement when he heard one. He was using the "power of silence" here to let Tony sell himself.

" . . . Probably should run a test," Tony mumbled. "Let me talk to Lew about it . . . leave me one of those sleeves you've got."

Jim took a calculated risk. Tony had the respect of Lew Taylor, and Mr. Taylor might agree to a test. On the other hand, Lew Taylor might turn it down. Then Jim would be faced with making an "end run" on Tony to get in and make his own presentation to Mr. Taylor. Right now, he had the goodwill of Tony. Jim and I had talked a lot about how inoffensive boldness pays off. He used a bit of it right here.

"Tony, I need a favor," Jim said. "Would you introduce me to Lew Taylor? I'd like to go over some of these things with both of you. The reason is that he just might have a question, maybe something on cost, maybe something on weight . . . I don't know, but at least I'd be there with the two of you and you could have the answers right then. Or, if you'd rather, let me call and make an appointment with him and tell him I'm working with you on this. . . . "

"Well, let me see if he's in. Tell you what, we'll just walk down to his office and check."

Jim had guessed right. Tony wouldn't be afraid to introduce us. We walked through those same swinging doors, down a hall to a plush carpeted area, and stopped at a secretary's desk.

"Ella," Tony asked, "is Lew tied up? I want him to meet a couple of people."

"Let me check." She walked to his door. "He said come on in."

"Thanks."

We followed Tony into a medium-size office with blond furniture. It had a sofa at one end facing Lew Taylor's desk. Somewhat to the side of his desk was a large overstuffed chair. Tony introduced us. Lew stood up, shook hands, motioned us to sit down with a gesturing toward the sofa. That isn't the best place to sell from: you're low, and too far away from the person on the other side of the desk, but there wasn't any choice in this case. Maybe it was best

Tony took the chair near the desk. Hopefully, he would do most of the selling.

Tony got right to the point and did a good job. He respected Lew Taylor, but wasn't afraid of him. He explained the cushion idea at the corners . . . how it was made with clusters of tear-shaped plastic bubbles. Jim got up and handed his sample to Tony. I thought that was smart, giving it to Tony rather than interrupting Tony and directly showing it to Lew. Lew was a tall man, rather quiet in manner, with warm, steady eyes.

I noticed that the papers on his desk were in neat, evenly placed piles. There were little weights on each pile. This was a very precise person, probably careful in making any changes. I wondered if Jim noticed. It would certainly make a difference in the presentation. This man would not tolerate vagueness. He would also be turned off to any generalities or exaggerations.

Lew Taylor fiddled with the cushion sleeve a bit. He asked me about the prices. I answered that Jim had the information on that; I simply worked for his company as a marketing consultant.

He turned to Tony. "Tony, these consultants are all over the place. I think we're missing out on a good thing."

Everyone laughed. Then he turned to Jim. "How much for these sleeves?"

"Of course it depends on the size. But let me give you an example for the twenty-four- by eighteen-inch boards you're packaging out there right now."

Jim went through various quantity prices. Then he made a smart move. He brought up the objection that Lew Taylor probably had on his mind . . . slowing down the packaging time by having to insert sleeves. Also, he gave credit to Tony, using the "recognition" motivation.

"But there's another cost, Mr. Taylor. Mr. Goss was good enough to go over the importance of time efficiency at the various stations, which apparently is getting you excellent cost reductions."

Lew Taylor nodded slightly. He had laid the cushion sleeve on his desk rather than give it back to Jim. That was a good sign. Immediately giving it back might have indicated courteous rejection or disinterest. He then leaned back with his hands behind his neck, not a position of intense interest.

Jim went on. "Although those sleeves slip on quickly, it is one more motion in your packaging, which I realize would translate into time and cost per package. What I'm wondering, and I need

your input on this, is that if our Korner Kushions did in fact
substantially cut down on damaged returns, it might wipe out the
added packing time costs, and, in fact, show a very good bottom
line savings on overall production costs."

Tony followed with "Like I told them, Lew, I believe these
sleeves will definitely cut some damage, but when it comes to
bottom line, with all costs figured, I just don't know."

Just then one of the executives of the company poked his head
in, asked Lew a few questions, and they talked back and forth a bit.
The man leaned against the doorframe as he talked . . . an indication
of a little lack of confidence or possibly shyness. A tough habit to
break, but not a good one if you're hoping to be in control or
persuade others.

Lew was lighting his pipe. "Tell you what, let us kick this
around a bit, and we'll get back to you on it."

"Fine," Jim said. Then he paused and followed up with, "Mr.
Taylor, could I see some of the damaged returns?"

"Suppose so . . . where are they now, Tony?"

"We put 'em all in the room next to storage; Mike repairs or
throws them out, depending on the damage."

Jim knew he couldn't crowd Lew Taylor, or force a close. But
he needed to get Lew Taylor involved as he did Tony. This idea
seemed like the only thing open and it really paid off.

They walked back to where rows of boxes were stacked. Everything was clean and in order . . . a reflection of the vice-president of
production. They walked into a brightly lit room where a fellow in
white coveralls was working on some damaged boards.

"Oh, hi, Mr. Taylor . . . hi, Tony."

"Hi, Mike. Mike, how much damage are we getting on the
corners of the boards?" Lew asked.

"Let me show you eight packages we got back this morning."

"Eight! . . . Really, Mike."

"Yeah. About 75 percent have corner damage, like this one.
Then we get 'em like this one where the trucker has stacked
something very heavy or sharp on top."

"Which sizes get the most damage?" Lew asked.

"I'd have to go through them . . . no, wait a minute, I've got
'em all down in this book . . . yeah . . . well, mostly it's the larger
ones."

"Jim, get with Mike here, get some price quotes up on the sizes
where we're getting the worst damage."

"I'll have it for you in the morning."

"No, I've got a long meeting in the morning."

"How about 2:30?" Jim asked, "or how about lunch?"

"Well . . . that's all right with me," Lew answered. "Want to make it for lunch, Tony?"

"Fine," Tony replied.

"All right," Lew said, "let's go over to Charlie's . . . say, about 12:30." Then he turned to us, "Charlie's has great gumbo . . . good seafood."

"Sounds good," Jim said. "We'll be here at 12:30."

I had to compliment Jim on the way back. He had done such a good job of getting his prospects involved. He asked for things very directly . . . such as seeing the plant, seeing firsthand the damaged goods. The showmanship was good. In doing these things he not only got them involved, but also he helped them sell themselves. He appealed to recognition, pride of self-approval, and presumed gratification. Next step . . . commitment.

About noon the next day, we headed for Palmer Industries again. Jim was armed with proposals covering a sixty-day test to begin in ten days. In the proposal he included the figures he got from Mike for the past sixty days. He felt that his comparison test of two sixty-day periods would appeal to Lew Taylor's analytical mind. As we drove, it was obvious from Jim's manner that he felt comfortable with the way things were going. His product would very definitely cut the damage. He mentioned in the proposal that they run a time study to show increased packing time per box. He knew this really wouldn't amount to much. Most of the increased costs would actually be in Jim's materials. He was rather amused that there was so much concern about the speed of packaging and little discussion about the material cost of adding his Korner Kushions. Little did he suspect that problems lay just ahead on those material costs. We pulled into the parking area marked for visitors.

"We're early; we sure made good time. What'll we do, sit out here for a while?" Jim asked.

"Might as well, for a few minutes at least."

"Guess I ought to check these proposals. They turned out nicely, don't you think, each one personalized with a name. And I didn't forget Gary Clark. We may meet him today. Plus, I brought two extras."

"You're thinking, Jim."

"Son of a gun!"

"What's the matter?"

"A lousy typo . . . right in the first paragraph, and I had time this morning to check it and didn't."

"It'll happen every time. I finally learned to always get one other person to check through a proposal with you. At least, Jim, it's not in someone's name."

"Yeah, thank goodness for that. Let's go on in . . . it's twenty-five after."

We were the only ones in the lobby. Yesterday there were several others. I couldn't help comparing them to Jim. Jim had that well-groomed look all the way. Yet, he wasn't fancy; just clean-looking. To me, the clean look is the successful look, shoes and everything spotless, neat, clean-looking hair, bright, clean teeth, no bitten or dirty nails, no long sideburns, no extra bracelets or showy jewelry. Appearance does influence.

After talking to the receptionist Jim sat down next to me. "Wonder how far away Charlie's seafood place is." he said.

"Don't know."

"Guess I should offer to go in my car."

"You can offer," I said with a laugh, "but I can just see those birds trying to crawl into the backseat."

"Yeah, it is a bit cramped, but I do like that Z. It's a honey!"

Just then Tony walked into the lobby.

"Here they are," he said to another man who was with him. They walked up to us and he introduced Gary Clark, the purchasing agent.

"Gary's going with us," Tony explained. "Lew is jammed up today."

"I've been looking forward to meeting you," Jim said to Gary.

When we got into the parking area Tony motioned to his car.

"Come on. Let's go in mine." It was a four-door so it worked out fine. Jim and I got in the back, and we headed for Charlie's. The time spent driving to lunch with a prospect is always interesting. It can be quite jovial, with everyone relaxed and talking. Other times, for no reason, it's strained. There's an attempt at being relaxed, but it's a cover-up. Silences are broken by efforts to say gracious things, show interest in the other person, or find ways to be liked.

I think it has a lot to do with those "vibrations" each one of us gives off. If they're right, they seem to mesh with the others, and everything is easy harmony. You really feel it in the close proximity of a car. Best answer I've found is to do that daily programming about "having a good rapport with everyone I meet that day." It gets rid of extra concern about how relationships are going. Somehow, you feel more comfortable. Long silences don't worry you, and when you don't feel uptight others feel at ease.

I wondered if Jim had done his "mind programming" on the way to this call. We needed a bit of rapport. You could feel the tension as we made conversation, first about good seafood, then about some places where Tony liked to fish.

Gary Clark didn't say much. He was probably in his forties, of medium height, and balding a bit. By the lines in his face he looked like an outdoorsman. He'd probably make a good model for one of those cigarette billboard ads showing a macho man near a mountain stream. Chances are some of the tension was due to his being called into this buying situation late. Jim was going to have to build some kind of a bridge with this man. It was a tough turn that Lew Taylor wasn't there. They had built a good relationship in a short time.

Charlie's seafood place was enjoyable. No loud music, lots of nautical gear on the walls. You couldn't help but think everything would be good. The atmosphere immediately had its relaxing effect. Even Gary broke into a big smile as the waiter put silly-looking bibs on all of us. After we ordered Tony opened up the business discussion.

"Let me kind of review where we are." He looked at Jim and me. "Buying is Gary's department. As I explained to him, we've been getting too many damaged returns. I think this really hit Lew yesterday. So whether we use your sleeves, whether we use more packing that we have . . . or use it differently, I don't know. We have to do something. Added material costs is a big factor. With that in mind, why don't you give Gary an idea of what you have and the prices."

Jim opened with a "status compliment." If it's sincere, it's one of the best in lowering resistance.

"Well, to begin with, Gary, you're up on the latest state-of-the-art in packaging products . . . so I'm not going to bore you with how this Korner Kushion is made." He handed the sample to Gary.

"Uh huh." Gary examined it, then gave it back to Jim. "Gardner has one that's very similar."

"Right," Jim answered, "I guess I've run into theirs now and then, and also Hobart's sleeve."

Jim and Gary were sparring a bit. Gary was trying to lower Jim's "expectancy" by immediately handing the sample back and also mentioning a similar product on the market. But Jim, by mentioning even another, was trying to show that Gary's remark didn't bother him.

"Gary, let me show you something quickly, before the food gets here."

He took the presentations out and handed them all around. Normally, he might have waited because he knew they'd be interrupted with the food in a minute. But he wanted to get a bit more rapport with Gary. Even such a small thing as his name being on the presentation might help. Also, he needed to establish the homework that was done on the various sized boards.

"These are the figures I got from Mike, Gary. Here are the damage results of the past sixty days."

"Can these be right, Tony?" It was obvious that Gary was surprised.

"Mike keeps pretty good records on what comes back. Of course, Gary, there's a lot that's minor in there, something that can easily and quickly be cleaned up."

"Sure, but every time there's a return you've got a loss of customer goodwill," Gary replied.

That gave Jim an opening. "That's a good point. One of our customers, Consolidated, went through the same thing. Lots of minor damage. But they switched over to us because the customer loss was hurting them."

The food came. Everyone was into the seafood platters. Later, lingering over coffee, Gary shot the first objection at Jim.

"Jim, you know that we've been using Emerald."

"Uh huh, they've got a good product line."

"With the quantities we buy, we're getting good discounts. I think the prices you've got listed here are just too high. Emerald's got a foam they use for corners . . . I think it's called "Emerald-Tuff" or something like that. I don't have the prices with me, but I'm sure they would beat yours, particularly with the discounts we've been getting."

That's always a tough objection. Someone doesn't have the facts, but they're sure they can beat your price. Jim didn't bristle. He nodded slightly, with a pleasant, interested look on his face.

"Gary, I don't blame you for considering that. Your job is to get the lowest prices for what's needed. I'm familiar with Emerald-Tuff. It's good, particularly with such things as shipping file cabinets. United is one of our customers. They had to cut their damaged returns and ran tests on four lines. They checked Saturn, Hackendorf, Emerald, and ours. They settled on ours because of price, and it came out first in their impact tests. Jimmy Colling in purchasing sent me this copy of the comparison . . . said it was okay for me to show to anyone. Interesting, isn't it? Now, for their heavy stuff, they use foam, possibly Emerald's, I don't know. Your shipments, however, are under fifty pounds per package. For the best protection, at the least cost for anything under fifty pounds, it is this . . . "

Jim picked up his Korner Kushion and went through the demonstration that he had given Tony the day before. Gary was much more interested than he had been before lunch. The reaction was good. He was examining the sleeve quietly. Jim was getting ready to close.

"You just saw how strong that sleeve is. Yet, notice how little space it takes. Trouble with foam is that it's bulky. You might have to go to larger-size boxes. That's one reason United didn't want to use it; it would have increased their box cost. As you said earlier, cost is a primary factor."

Jim was making good use of the third-person testimonial, and the "as-you-said-earlier" is a great deflator of objections. Gary seemed to have half a smile on his face . . . seasoned purchasing agents enjoy a sales professional in action.

Jim went on, "Gary, Tony, this little sleeve right here is going to save you money. It certainly did for United, for Sanford Shippers, American, Mid-West, and I feel we can do the same for you. At the end of this sixty-day test, you two, Lew Taylor, and Mike with his records, you're going to sit down and take a hard look at the results of your decision. I think you're going to be pleasantly surprised with the money you're saving Palmer Industries.

"All I need from you is your okay and we'll have this test going on all four lines by Thursday of next week. And, personally, I'd like to work with both of you."

Jim had just used the gracious "tail out" in asking for the business. And he was now doing the toughest thing of all . . . keeping quiet. He was waiting for them to break the silence. To add anything would dilute the strength of those closing statements. He kept quiet.

"What do you think, Gary?" Tony asked.

"Well . . . "

"I think it's what we need," Tony interrupted. "And I think it will be easy to handle on my production line."

"Then we ought to go ahead and make the bulk buy," Gary said. "Get the lowest price rather than the sixty-day test quantity. If it doesn't work, we wouldn't continue anyway."

"Yeah, I guess you're right."

Gary was pondering. You could almost see the wheels turning.

"Look, Jim," he said. "Give 5 percent off that bulk price and you've got yourself a deal."

Jim took a moment, then replied, "Gary, I'd love to, but if we did that we'd have to go back to all our customers and rebate them. We couldn't stay in business if we did that. Certainly if you were one of those customers you wouldn't like it."

"Nobody'd have to know."

"I'd know."

Gary laughed. "Just wanted to see where your bottom line was, Jim. When we get back to the plant I'll give you a purchase order."

"Okay, so who's going to take care of the check?" Tony kidded.

"Now that," Jim said, "I can handle without rebating our customers."

They all laughed.

13

Negotiating Strategy

*P*ower is influence over others. You are probably using this influence to negotiate something every day. You and someone else are making concessions. Ideally, both feel good about the results. It could be as simple as being in the wrong lane in heavy traffic when you see the road narrows up ahead. Instead of trying to "force" your car in, making another driver angry and feeling contempt or guilt yourself, you lower the window, smile at the driver and make a signal that you want in. Most drivers will then graciously give you space. You gave this driver the concession of a smile and respect. The driver gave you the concession of stopping to let you in, a small act of persuasion on your part where you both felt good about the outcome.

You're into negotiating with your children when they're allowed to do something they want when they've finished their homework. It goes on with wife and husband, employee and employer. You may ask for a better seat at a restaurant, a better price at a hotel, a better lease agreement, some additional service or terms when you purchase something. A politician is constantly trading off concessions. And so it goes, on up to international summit meetings.

The salesperson is up against trained negotiators. Sitting across the desk from the prospect, he feels the pressure of possibly losing the business on price. Underneath that poised appearance is the gnawing pressure that his company, miles away, is expecting him to get the business, and get it at the right price.

Negotiating can be one of the most rewarding experiences in persuading another. It can also bring out the worst in tactics when a person is blinded by pride, ego, fear, or simply the desire for approval. Results of a negotiating session can leave a person feeling like a winner. It can also carry a distressful aftertaste of anxiety and guilt over the outcome. Perhaps one of the all-time classics in terrible negotiating was Chamberlain of England in negotiating with Hitler to halt further aggression. That negotiating farce changed the course of history.

Your negotiating should be exhilarating . . . a challenging and uplifting experience. The results should leave you and the other party feeling good about the outcome.

The Results of High Expectancy

The foremost mistake that most negotiators make is having too low an expectation. To be successful in negotiating you must push your expectancy level up. In persuading others, keep this in mind. Sharp negotiators can make you anxious and lower your expectancy. In his book, *Give & Take*, Chester L. Karrass explains that in controlled experiments with business people, the inexperienced negotiator with a high expectancy level outperformed the experienced negotiator with a low expectancy level.

In advertising, go after the twelve-month contract if you hope to settle for six months. Start high in expectations. In leasing, go after five years. You just might get it, although you have a bottom line of three years. In fact, to be at the top in selling you absolutely must start high. In price negotiations your experienced buyer is going to start very low. Therefore, you must have room—lots of it—in which to negotiate. That way both parties come away feeling like winners.

High Performance Is Facing Rejection Head On!

Successful negotiating is taking risks. Most people fear rejection. That includes your competition. They fear it. They run from it . . . and are therefore running away from the big orders. Rejection is part of the price on the way to high achievement. It's the same in any field. In one game a professional quarterback may get both boos and cheers from people who take little risk and make only a fraction of what he makes. A salesclerk behind the counter simply fills orders with little risk of rejection. As a creative salesperson, you're in a different arena. Your compensation is much higher. It wouldn't be if there were no risk of rejection.

You risk rejection when you ask for a purchase order number, ask to see the president, ask for *all* the business, stand firm on your price, ask for an exclusive contract. You risk rejection when you ask why you are not being considered, ask to refigure the bid after a turndown, when you go back after the business following a series of turndowns. You're taking a risk when you do something highly imaginative to get the business. Certainly, you risk rejection when you make an end run on a purchasing agent after all attempts for the business have failed.

Tap Your Resources for Keen Insights

Along with risk-taking, bank heavily on your intuition. For example, you're about to make an important callback on a prospect. Your previous call showed interest and you are going back with a proposal. To get the commitment, there will probably be some negotiating.

Before making that important call be alone for about five or ten minutes. Sit and relax your body. This may be difficult at your office. There may be phone interruptions, or you may be self-conscious that someone will pop in and see you just sitting there, "not working." Your car may be the best idea. Pull into a shopping area and park for a few minutes.

Now go into Deep Alpha as explained earlier. Let your subconscious feed you vital information. Let that intuition tool work for you. Don't pass up this part in your selling and persuading efforts. The temptation will be, "I know it's a good idea, but today I don't have much time. Maybe tomorrow." Getting yourself to do this takes a bit of self-discipline. I know. I've put it off, not done it, even though I know how critical it is to a successful negotiation.

Right now you may be thinking, "Come on, Patton, I'm into negotiating many times during the day. What do I do before each meeting, go find some place to park and meditate?" If it's an important piece of negotiating, yes. That would be the smartest use of time you could make. In an office building, to be alone I've resorted to the privacy of the men's room for ten minutes. There are many times in the course of selling when there's negotiating. Certainly you're not going to jump up and ask where the rest rooms are during the meeting.

After you've "let the tensions drain out of your fingers and your toes" pose some questions to yourself either out loud or silently. Then wait a bit to see what bubbles forth from the subconscious. All resulting thoughts will not be profound. Some will be idle thoughts. But you'll quickly recognize those gems of insight and strategy.

Here is a group of suggested questions you might ask yourself:

1. Can this person make the final decision? If not, would it be wiser to put the meeting off until all concerned are available?
2. What do I know about this person? What about ego needs, income, ambition, life-style, probable weaknesses, strengths, habits, self-esteem, interests? Who and what might this person be afraid of? Whom would this person most likely want to impress? What would this person most want to hide?
3. What facts do I need to find out? How, and do I have time?
4. What will be this person's hope or probable expectancy in this negotiation? How can I lower the expectancy level yet maintain interest?

Example: Jane Mulloy walked into E. L. Eaton's office with high expectancy. He was head of marketing for a large, well-known department store in Dallas. She sold radio time for a station that appealed to the upper-income audience, so it was a natural for Mr. Eaton to use.

But Mr. Eaton also had high expectancy. He expected to break the rate card by dangling the possibility of heavy saturation. He also expected these low-cost announcements to be placed in high-priced drive time.

When Mr. Eaton told her what he wanted she didn't show any concern. She explained how the staff at the radio station were all excited about the idea of working with Mr. Eaton's store; that although they couldn't come off the rate card they would do everything possible to schedule the announcements in the times Mr. Eaton would want. She said, however, that there was a problem. The availability of drive time was very tight. But she would see what could be moved.

Mr. Eaton countered with the fact that they were "looking at other stations."

She said she could certainly understand that . . . if she were doing the buying, she would want the best rates possible.

She remembered that one of Mr. Eaton's peeves was how close competitive announcements were on TV and radio stations. So she gave him the clincher. In exchange for the long-term schedule the station would keep his announcements at least eighteen minutes away from any competition, instead of the usual policy of ten minutes. Mary got a heavy saturation contract at regular rates. Mr. Eaton got the audience he wanted plus a concession on commercial scheduling.

5. What might the competition be offering? What is their usual pattern in any negotiating? Do I know the competitive reps, their expertise, and their usual behavior in making concessions? What are the reps' strong and weak points? If I worked for the competition, what would I do or say to get the business?

6. What are the three key benefits the prospect will get from buying this? Could one of these be a high ego benefit . . . a benefit that would make the prospect look good or important in the eyes of another person, or make the prospect feel good about him or herself? If so, what "rationalization excuses" can I give this person, "reason why" facts that the person can explain to others.

   An example might be a president okaying the purchase of a company airplane, with the rationalization being they can increase orders, save time, and so on. In all selling and negotiating, keep this truism in mind: *Logic and reason ride the horse of emotion*!

7. Factual features are always tied to emotional benefits. But to give these credibility, there should be *proof*!

   What proof can I offer? What companies or people can I quote as saying they are very happy with the service or product? What do I have in printed form that backs up the facts and benefits with the "power of legitimacy?"

8. Exactly how far will I go in giving away concessions? What is absolutely my bottom line? Knowing this beforehand is so important. It is easy to be emotionally swayed to give too much either through fear of losing the order, or because of the charismatic influence of the buyer.

   Example: Leroy Calkins sells wallboard. He was on his fourth callback to a hard-nosed contractor. The contractor kidded around with Leroy for a while before getting down to business. Then he suggested they have some coffee. The contractor motioned to a sofa chair and coffee table in a corner of his large office.

   As Leroy sank into the expensive sofa he felt a kind of euphoria. Then the contractor said, "You know, Leroy, we're going to be buying lots of wallboard. But Leroy, I need your help today. I can give you a good order, but we bid way too low on a job, so

I really need your cooperation on this one. . . . I just can't go with the prices we've been talking about."

The contractor charmed Leroy into a bad loss on the order plus taking an extended time to pay for it.

9. What objections am I likely to run into? What will I counter with? What hidden objection might there be?

10. What would their "bottom line" be? Ask yourself, if I were in their shoes, what would be the top price I'd pay? what extras would I want? what concessions other than price would really appeal to me? What tactics would I use with this salesperson to lower the expectancy level, instill fear, get extra concessions in payment terms, storage, shipping, or trade, or in some exclusive rights or advertising allotment?

11. What are all the possible concessions that I could make? Remember, a small concession to you may be important to someone else. Out of these concessions, which one is interesting and dramatic? This is the one that you may want to hold for the close.

12. Where's the showmanship? What can I use to dramatically make a point? What can I show? What would have emotional impact? How many different senses can I appeal to?

Team Negotiating

If you are making the call with another person, perhaps your sales manager, marketing person, project or design engineer, mentally go through a game plan. Who is going to carry the ball? If it is you, let them know when, how, and why you are going to temporarily hand it off to them, and when and how they must toss it back to you.

Don't overlook the opportunity to build the other person up. We can't brag about ourselves in front of a prospect, but someone else can. And if this is really an important meeting with a lot at stake, rehearse it at least three times with someone really knowledgeable playing the role of the tough buyer. Effective? You bet. Ask any trial lawyer. They're selling. And they wouldn't think of not going through a realistic role play with someone playing the devil's advocate.

One thing: If you do take someone along, have a good reason for doing so. Another person, in an effort to be friendly or helpful, may start talking about something irrelevant just as you're smoothly heading into a final point of commitment.

Program Your Mental Attitude

Program your mind before the meeting. After you've gone through the self-questions program your mind for positive results. Doing this one thing makes such a difference on how you come across.

On the way to the meeting repeat several times out loud: "He and I or she and I are going to get along great. . . . we'll have a good, warm rapport!" Say it several times in your own choice of words. Feel it. Try to get some caring emotion in that feeling. Any strong animosity toward any person you're going to meet with can hurt you. Little undercurrent thoughts of dislike attract negative results.

I'm not talking about being goody-goody or sweet. You can be quite competitive, very strong, even have emotional outbursts, and be quite positive. Your attitude profile is one of strength and caring with warm humor, high expectancy, and a keen understanding of human nature and needs.

Making Concessions

Studies of hundreds of negotiating events showed the primary flaw of even experienced negotiators was that they did not know the real needs or emotional wants of the other party. Most of them felt that the specific wants of the other party were about the same as their own. Also, these very experienced negotiators thought that the other person put the same value on a concession that they had.

In reality, the other party often has different wants from the negotiator. Wants are emotional cravings. You sense these cravings by observing the person, the person's manner, listening much more than talking, thinking how they would fit on the DESAnalysis, and asking questions.

You're looking for some sensing feedback: Where is the prospect vulnerable? What fears does he probably have? Does he seem security conscious? Does he seem like a risk-taker? By his dress, manner, material possessions, and talk, do you feel he is quite vain? Would prestige probably be important to him? Is he family oriented? What do you feel he really wants? What do you think his company wants? What do you think he thinks the company wants?

Concessions can be other than money and services. A concession has perceived value by the other person. You are giving a concession when you listen. You are actually giving a concession with a smile, with patience, by giving helpful knowledge. Remember, we are dealing with what satisfies another person's wants and needs.

Example: A salesman for a medical supply company was bidding on a $250,000 piece of equipment to a hospital. He found out about a special new service the hospital was trying out, called the newspaper, and got them to do a story. The publicity was a concession much appreciated by the administrator. The salesman got the bid and the full price on the equipment.

Giving information away freely is giving away power. Make it count as a concession. The sharp buyer-negotiator is listening to your talk about the quota your company has set for you, or any financial tidbit about your company that could be used to gain an advantage in price.

Increase your power with good information. Use questions and use your eyes. Really see. Top salespeople know vast amounts of information about the companies they call on. A sales engineer has little trouble gaining rapport with another engineer and will usually glean all kinds of information that may help get a bid through. This is one of the reasons many purchasing agents don't want salespeople roaming the plant talking to nonnegotiating-type people.

Inventory Your Power

Get acquainted with your negotiating power. Time is power . . . make yours count. Your contacts are power. Your position, length of time with your company, wealth, status, credentials, interests, influence with your company, knowledge, memory, ability to articulate, formulate things on paper, health, positive attitude, age, appearance, image, imagination . . . all can be power sources.

Negotiating is leveraging your power. You'll see the subtle ways it can be used in the next chapter.

14

Negotiating Tactics

Your strategy started in your mind. By posing questions to yourself, your intuition and imagination helped form a plan. By mentally conditioning the quality of your thoughts, you have put into play forces that influence your behavior, plus the receptive behavior of the other person.

What tactics will you use? What tactical changes could and should you make? Although these are considered from a salesperson's standpoint, they can be applied to selling yourself to a prospective employer, selling your present employer on a raise, or any area where you are trying to persuade another.

Let's look at a number of ideas that you can use.

Changing Locations Changes the Climate

When you seem deadlocked in a negotiation, or if there seems to be irritation, change locations. Find something to change. Try going out for lunch or dinner or some place for coffee or a drink. It is amazing how the entire climate can change to friendship as one exchanges information about family, hobbies, or business. If the prospect won't change locations, then change your seat, go to the bathroom, or ask him if he has change for a Coke. When in an impasse get the person to do something for *you* . . . something easy, of course.

The Flinch Tactic

Negotiators use this in varying degrees to make the other person feel out of line, or a bit small. You are letting the other person know they have gone too far. For example, your prospect may make a very low price request. Your reaction could be, "Aw, come on now!" It might be a startled look, a grimace, an outright laugh showing disbelief, or a rolling of the eyeballs. Of course, buyers may use this on you when you quote a price: "What! You've got to be kidding." An employer may use the flinch in response to a raise request by an employee. This calculated tactic quickly lowers the "expectation level."

Using the Power of Legitimacy

People tend to believe anything in print. We have been conditioned to this at an early age. Numerous psychological tests back this up. This gives any price quotation the "power of legitimacy" if it is in print. The printed price is an effective starting point for a negotiation. As a seller, keep this in mind and test anything on a sign or in print. For example, there may be a sign in a purchasing agent's outer office stating that salespeople are seen only on Tuesdays and Thursdays. Even the purchasing agent's secretary may believe it. Test it. Try for the other days when you don't have to wait. I used to make a practice of this and only once had to make the call on the stated day. Keep a healthy skepticism regarding any so-called fact you see in print. As a negotiating tool for yourself, do invest in good typesetting for warrantees, prices, bulletins, regulations, and sheets proclaiming the virtues of yourself and your company.

Go in High

The prospect must come away from the negotiation feeling he or she has won something. Going in high and coming down, but not too easily or quickly, gives that winning feeling. It is an absolute must in real estate. Certainly do this in going after a job, or asking for a raise. A good technique is to stand in front of a mirror beforehand and ask out loud for what you want seven times. This practice will assure you that when you are face to face with the other person the figure will come out without the slightest faltering or change in your voice or change in your facial expression or any downward glance.

The Time Tactic

We humans resist change. We may not always like the way things are. But the mind is "comfortable" with the status quo. So, when you propose a new concept you must expect some resistance. You must let a person get used to your idea. In the brain of that person many new neuron connections must be made. As you continue to propose your idea over a period of time, those first connections between the neurons are being reinforced by new connections. Outright rejection changes to possible consideration. Consideration may then change to full acceptance. The other person's brain is now "comfortable" with your new idea.

This is one of the reasons the average sale is made after the fifth callback. The prospect must feel "comfortable" with this new person—you. In negotiating we must develop patience and not let initial rejection discourage us or change our course of direction. Time lets people get used to new ideas. They must have this time. Most of us are too impatient and don't allow for this period of "getting used to an idea." Russian negotiators are masters at this time tactic.

Bracketing to a Higher Figure

A person may be thinking of a certain price for what you are selling. That figure may be far to low. This frequently happens with such things as property, leases, or consulting services. If you suspect this, it might be wise in the course of the presentation to move your prospect's thinking to a higher probable price. Otherwise when you do get to the final price, it may be so much higher than what the person had in mind that the shock is too great to overcome.

If you suspect this, you can change a prospects' thinking to the possibility of a very high figure. This is bracketing. One way this can be done is to summarize all the services that you are going to perform. Then state, or better yet, show on paper, that if all this were done separately, the total price would come to a certain figure. That figure is the high bracket you wish to plant. Then you explain through "packaging the way we're doing it" the total investment would be a certain figure, which is lower than the high figure you put in their mind. Yet, it is actually higher than the initial low price that they were thinking.

In real estate this "conditioning" is sometimes done by quoting "comps." These are quotes of prices of other "comparable" pieces of property that have sold in that area. Those late-night TV hard-sell commercials almost always use a form of bracketing. The announcer extolls the virtues of a complete set of pans, then throws in a complete set of utensils hoping to condition you to a $90 figure.

Then comes the figure: $29.95, "if you act right now." In all bracketing the object is to change the expectation of what you will probably pay or should be paying, then give you a lower figure.

The Silence Tactic

Use it. It's powerful. Also recognize when it is being used on you. Controlled silence makes people come up with the second answer. The second answer is usually closer to the truth. Let's say you're negotiating store space in a shopping strip. The prospect says he doesn't want to pay that much per foot. Complete silence on your part. After the long pause the prospect says, "What's bothering me is that restaurant. Their customers may take up all the parking area." You have gotten to the real objection with the use of silence. You might then show how other stores have had no problem; that the restaurant, in fact, provided more walk-in trade, and so on.

Some prospects use silence beautifully. You quote a price. They just stare at you or look down in silence. Unnerved, some salespeople come up with a new price. More silence. A concession is added.

GAMES SOME BUYERS PLAY

Limited Authority

Frequently, the buyer can, in fact, make the decision on the proposal. But the tactic of not having the authority buys time to weigh your proposal against another or seek opinions from others. Sometimes they explain that they'll have to take it up with the buying committee. This can exert unnerving pressure on a salesperson who may come up with additional concessions.

Of course, you, the salesperson, can do the same. You can't approve a certain concession, must take it to a higher up. This gives it more value.

The Build-up Tactic

A buyer compliments you, your organization, product, or service. The product or service is given real value. Psychologically you may feel inclined to give some "concession" in return. Then you are asked if you could possibly reduce the price. The justification might be that the person will send business your way.

EXAMPLE: A woman attorney in Denver found the exact fur coat she wanted. The price was $7,000. She went by the store a number of times. Each time she would try on the coat. And each time she complimented the furrier on the quality of the store and that particular fur. Finally, in a warm and friendly way, she let him know she wanted that fur; certainly it was well worth it. Then she asked him to do something for her on the price. Next, she bluntly said that she had many contacts with affluent people and would certainly be sending them to him. She got the coat for $5250.

The Tear-down Tactic

The buyer wants your product or service but must reduce your expectancy level. In real estate this could be mentioning the loud traffic on the street, the long distance to schools, or silently rubbing a finger over some cracks you thought he wouldn't see.

One buyer I know uses two big, fat folders to do this. When he's really interested in buying something he'll pull out both folders and wave them at the salesperson. Then he'll ask, "You know what these are? These are people who want to sell me what you're selling. And many of them are tops in the industry. So if you want an order, you're going to have to really sweeten the price."

Put Your Boss on the Spot

Bringing in your boss can be a good tactic in exerting power with a buyer or in getting higher up, such as having your boss meet the buyer's boss. However, a shrewd buyer may find this is the time to make demands. There is no letting you get extra time with a limited authority tactic here. Also, the buyer knows your boss wants to look good to you by wrapping up the deal then and there. So the buyer may ask for some tough concessions.

High-quantity Price on a Small Order

EXAMPLE: You're elated over the proposed one hundred boxcar order. So is your boss. You gave the bottom price for such a large order. When the order comes through it is for one boxcar but at the one hundred boxcar low price. The explanation is that that was all they needed at this moment. It turns out that that is the only order you receive from the company.

Your "Specs" as a Leverage

Your "specs" are used to get lower prices from other vendors. Much work may go into special specifications and pricing for a prospect. Callbacks inform you that no decision has been made. Information gets back to you that your specs were looked at by other vendors to determine whether they could do the same but at a lower cost. You did all the initial work in formulating the specifications.

Walk Out

This is a great tactic in negotiating. A buyer may, in effect, "walk out" on you by saying he's sorry but if that's the best you can do they'll deal with someone else. Keep going back with "throwaway" concessions, or possibly some imaginative concession other than price. This walk-out tactic is calculated to force your price. Of course, you can use it as a salesperson. You simply say, "I'm sorry, that's as low as I can go" . . . and walk away. Then you return later with a concession other than price.

Your Information as Leverage with Present Vendor

Your company receives a letter that a firm is open for bids on a project that might use your product or service. There is usually a deadline. You work to get the bid in on time. It may be quite legitimate. But some companies are using this to get all kinds of vendor information. They may use the information to put pressure on their present vendor to come down in price. They may have little intention of changing vendors. But it is a pressure that often works.

EXAMPLES OF TACTICS

Suppose you are selling computers in a computer store. A prospect walks in and inquires about a certain computer. The customer balks at your price. You carefully go over the features and benefits. The customer buys. You closed the sale, but there was no negotiating.

Now, suppose the customer said he was going to buy a computer, but he was also going to check out your competitor down the street. Although he made the first concession by saying he was going to buy, he also exerted a form of power frequently used by buyers; he used the tactic of fear that he might buy from another . . . the *threat of competition*.

You have a few power tactics of your own. You are going to lower the other person's *expectancy level*. First, your body language, words, or manner do not disclose that this power threat had any effect on you. In fact, you come back with your own ploy.

In a friendly manner you let him know that you don't blame him for wanting to get the best price. Then you let him know how fast this particular computer is selling. You may wish to insert a few truthful anecdotes naming some customers who compared prices and features, decided on your computer, and how happy they are with the benefits. You might *reinforce credibility* by offering the phone numbers of several of these customers.

Information gives you a negotiating edge. You ask him some questions. What will he use it for? Who else will use it? He discloses that his bookkeeper likes this particular model; also, he's leaving town in the morning. If he did decide on it, could it be delivered this afternoon? Your prospect has given away several important pieces of power: the bookkeeper likes it, and he, the prospect, is leaving town and he wants to make a decision before he leaves. This *deadline information* works to your advantage. Eighty percent of negotiating is done in the last 20 percent of any time frame.

Generally, try not to be the first in giving a concession. In this case, the prospect gave away the first by saying he was going to buy a computer and followed with other information concessions. Frequently, a salesperson is in a position where he must give the first concession. Also, a small first concession may melt some barriers and spark interest in further negotiating.

Try to *give worth to every concession*, however small. You are now going to give away your first concession, but not too easily. You want it to be very worthwhile to the other person. Remember how a classy jeweler displays his product? Your voice and manner come into play here. You let him know that normal delivery would be next Tuesday. However, you're going to check with the manager to see what can be done to get it out there this afternoon.

You could have made that decision, but you added worth to it by exercising *limited authority*. There are other advantages to limited authority. Although you wouldn't need it in this example, many times limited authority buys you time or lets you press for concessions from the other person, but without the authority to give concessions on your own part.

In all negotiating *ask for concessions*. The prospect is doing this when he tells you to put a good price on it, and you may do some business. His *concession* is that he will buy. You come back with a concession. You let him know the discount for cash. He says you'll have to do better than that. He is using what is known as the *crunch*. A clever negotiator can keep coming back with that same "you'll have to do better than that" answer every time you give a price.

Now you're going to do a little *escalating*. Would he be needing a printer? His answer is that he might if you come up with a good price on the package. He is exerting negotiating *power*.

You are now going to make a *concession*. You let him know that you can probably work something out. But in order to get a good discount from Mr. Emory, the manager, you need to submit it in order form. You are attempting to get *commitment*. You are also taking some *risk*. He could refuse and thus take some power from you. By letting you go ahead he has *transferred power* to you. And you are again using the tactic of *limited authority*. Mr. Emory will have to okay the discount. Also, you are being *slow* in giving the discount concession, and by making it a bit harder to get you are giving it more *worth*, thus giving the prospect a *winning feeling*.

The manager okays a nice discount. You start to wrap up the sale. But the prospect thinks that possibly he wants the larger, letter-quality printer. In fact, he's sure he wants the more expensive letter-quality printer. Now he's going to use the *"bogey tactic."* He wants it, but he explains he has only a limited amount of budget for both the printer and computer. You explain the installment plan. He does not want to pay the interest. You both stand there. He says nothing, hoping the tactic of *silence* will move you to a further concession. You don't buy the silence tactic, so he will try the *walk-away tactic*. He shrugs and says something about looking elsewhere. Now, you are well aware of your *downside* or *bottom line* limits. You have just a small amount of bargaining room left in the price. But you have some software concessions that you haven't used. First, though, you're going to use the *power of legitimacy* by showing him the printed price list for both the computer and the printer. You have now established further *worth* to the discount you gave him.

Now you are going to give him a *dramatic concession* to wrap up the sale. Earlier, he had mentioned that he was going to also use the computer himself for organizing presentations. He *transferred power* to you with this information. Now you let him know you can't cut the price any further, but you will include a special word processing software package that sells for $495 and is excellent for organizing and writing presentations.

Next you use the tactic of *summarizing* the concession list. You explain that in addition to the no charge for the software you will give him the discount you got approved, plus get it specially delivered this afternoon at no extra charge.

He agrees, but wants to look over the various word processing software. He picks up the most expensive word processing software package, the one that includes spelling correction, not the one you were planning to give him.

He tells you that's the one he wants. He is doing what is called *cherry-picking*. And as he's about to write the check he pauses and does a little *nibbling*. "Hey, with a sale like this how about including a carton of floppy disks?"

You're both happy. *You both won.* He feels he won some good concessions. You feel good because you sold a high-price package and didn't have to give away too much.

That is the essence of good negotiating; both parties have won. But what did each win? Not the computer/printer package. Not the money from that package. Your customer got a *wants fulfillment*. And, as the seller, you received a *wants fulfillment*. This is a must in good negotiating.

In this case the buyer *wanted* to feel good about himself in running an efficient office. He may have *wanted* to look important to friends, or even the bookkeeper, or perhaps his wife, who would talk about the computer to her friends. He *wanted* to *feel* important. Perhaps he *wanted* to visualize himself as a fast-track entrepreneur . . . with his office centered around the latest in technology. Buying that special computer was a means to that end. He needed to *win*. You let him feel like a *winner* by getting those concessions.

As the seller, you *wanted* to feel good about yourself. Certainly you wanted the commission. But more important, you needed to feel you were a *winner*. We all *want* that feeling. This customer let you feel that way. You will *feel* important as you tell your wife about the sale. And if you have a good month you *visualize* buying that special car you want and how you will *look* driving it.

After the customer left you might have gone right into the manager's office and let him know the sale was wrapped up. Actually, you wrapped up *being a winner*. You might even brag a bit about how you captured a sale that was on its way to a competitor down the street. And if your manager was a good one, he would have listened intently and approvingly helping you satisfy that *want of approval*.

He has strong wants too. He *wants* to look good to the owner. Helping you get your satisfaction means your selling enthusiasm will remain high.

With more sales, the manager will satisfy *wants* not only to look good to the owner, but also to business friends and family, plus satisfy his own *wanting to win* and have *self-approval* . . . the need to feel smart. He was smart in hiring you; you've made him grow and *look good to others*.

AVOIDING MISTAKES

Jerry Higgins picked up the ringing phone. "Jerry . . . Mike Hanfield over at Arnold & Hanfield. Okay . . . we're going ahead with you on the 110,000 mail-outs with envelopes at $18,700 that you quoted . . . using the window envelope and the letter on classic laid like we talked about. I'll put a purchase order in the mail today."

Jerry was glowing a bit after hanging up. That was a nice order. But a couple of uneasy thoughts tried to creep in. In the past two weeks he had made a number of quotes. He didn't have the notes in front of him on this one; he knew they had talked about the quality of the paper, but did he include classic laid in the quote?

He found out later the quote was based on an inexpensive stock. In the past year he had learned a few things about negotiating the hard way.

1. Don't negotiate on the phone if you're not prepared with notes or a checklist.
2. Don't let other people's outbursts of emotions throw you. A person on the stand crying at the right time has moved more than one jury.
3. Before a negotiation think what is the *worst* and what is the *best* that can happen.

4. Interruptions can kill the progress of a negotiation. Try to choose a setting where this won't happen. Try to have the negotiation on your turf.

5. The biggest killer of negotiations is *ego*. Ask any real estate agent. Example: A person is asking $185,000 for a house. An interested buyer makes a very low offer of $145,000 just to test the price. The agent delivers the offer to the seller. The seller is insulted, and rants and raves at the agent for bringing in such a contract. Actually, he's hoping to get $170,000 for the house. Being angry, he counters with $182,000. This makes the prospective buyer, who was thinking of going as high as $172,000 angry. So, the prospective buyer tells the agent, "If that idiot thinks his house is worth so much, he can have it!"

6. Another ego problem: When a party of three consists of two men and one woman there may be problems because of the competitiveness of the male ego. If you run into problems of this type, the woman may do well to meet with each man individually. The same can happen with three men or three women, but it more frequently happens with two men and one woman.

7. Going in too low. Henry was being interviewed for a job. He needed $25,000 just to get by, and that's what he asked for. He was well qualified. The CPA firm would have gone to $30,000. He should have gone in with $32,000. Settling at the $30,000 figure both he and the company would have won. That ties in with number eight.

8. Failure to take risks. Without risk you do not win much. Keep that expectancy level up, up, up! And don't be afraid to start high.

9. Not cultivating influencers. These are the people who can pave the way for you by putting in a good word. These are the foremen, the engineers, the secretaries. These are people behind the scenes who can feed you vital information about the competition, about deadlines, about needs, about where the money would come from, the politics, about problems or the buying channels and method of purchasing.

10. Failure to know your bottom line and bottom line tangents. Ann was booking a large meeting for her hotel. They were looking at 300 people for three days. She was up against a price that another hotel had quoted. She needed bottom line commitment from her boss, from catering, some extra concessions of

limo service, gifts in each room, special free suites for the president and chairman of the board. In negotiating, the toughest but most important selling may be getting the needed cooperation in your own company.

11. Giving away a deadline while negotiating the price. Example: Martha was getting married the next day, but she had forgotten to order flowers for the church. She frantically called a florist and told them her plight before discussing price.

12. Listen with concern. Your listening time should be much greater than talking time. In negotiating listening and observing will keep you out of trouble. Too much talking can get you into trouble, can lessen your negotiating power.

13. Read the fine print. All of it. If you're the Expressive personality type, this particularly applies to you. You hate forms and contracts. You love people. You trust people. And, a suggestion to you impatient, impulsive Dominant types: Read it . . . all of it.

FORCES WORKING FOR YOU

The most important ingredients going for you in negotiating are your integrity, fair play, courage to take risks, and high expectancy, plus a warmth and respect toward the other person. If you throw those out and just go in with clever tactics, the gains will be short-lived.

It's a little like a tennis match. You try to be mentally tough. There are times you must take risks on a passing shot. And there are times when you'd like to call your opponent's ball out on a close line call. But like negotiating, there would be no gain if it wasn't with integrity. And throughout the tactics of finesse and competitiveness there is dignity and respect for the other person. With such an attitude, the forces of influence are working for you.

15

Thirty-three Questions and Answers

Q: How Important Is the Business Lunch?

A: It can be very productive in getting and holding good business. The advantage is informality and getting to know one another on a personal basis. You get a chance to find common interests and build rapport. There's a letting down of resistance in the pleasantness of a lunch, away from interruptions.

Q: Who Decides Where to Eat and When?

A: You, the seller, if you've made the invitation. It's usually a good idea to suggest a choice. If the prospect says it doesn't matter, quickly make the decision. Always call in a reservation. And unless the restaurant is crowded, tell them to give you a large table. You're the leader and you're seeing to your prospect's comforts. Definitely assert yourself regarding the position of the table. You can do this with a smile. You don't want to sit near loud groups, the kitchen, or rest-room doors.

Q: Should You Drink?

A: That's a personal decision, and it depends on the circumstances. You should ask if the prospect would care for a drink, regardless. If you're not planning to have one, you'll want to make the prospect feel comfortable about drinking alone. A statement such as, "How about something to drink? I'm going to pass right now, but what would be your pleasure?"

Drinks affect people differently. Two drinks on an empty stomach are too much for lunch. You may babble on and not realize you're talking too much. You won't be thinking clearly. It may blow the rest of the afternoon. If you ever overdrink, even slightly, cancel appointments. Definitely do not go back to your office. It will be noticed, and you may lose the respect of the employees.

Q: At Lunch, When Should You Start Talking Business?

A: The prospect will probably give you the cue on this. If the prospect seems to be enjoying light conversation, continue with it. Go with what feels comfortable or natural. You may get all the way through the meal and not take it up until the end. There are times when you sense it's best not to bring it up at all. You've simply developed a pleasant rapport for future business. Don't get the "guilties" on this one and think that just because it's on company expense you have to talk some business. Talking about that person's interests may be the best selling you could do.

A business breakfast has a great appeal to many busy executives. Generally, they would expect to get down to business very quickly at that time of day.

Q: What Do You Do if the Prospect Picks up the Check?

A: Certainly grab for it quickly. But if your prospect insists, graciously accept and thank him. You avoid any problem with this by quietly instructing the waiter in advance.

On the subject of checks: The majority of restaurants are terrible about making you wait for a check. This can be very aggravating to both you and your guest. To have it all flow smoothly, ask to have the check brought with the food. A busy prospect will appreciate this.

Q: As a Woman, How Do You Best Handle Picking up the Check?

A: If you're taking a man to lunch or dinner you need to discreetly let the waiter know he is to bring you the check. If there's any discussion with your prospect, let him know it's your treat. Another friendly way is: "This time it's my treat." In some cases you may wish to excuse yourself for the powder room and on the way take care of the bill.

Q: Is it Okay to Make Phone Calls When You're Out to Lunch with Someone?

A: Only a quick one to your office. Otherwise, no phone calls. It's an ego slight to be away from the table for an extended time. You're keeping others waiting while you're conducting business. You want that prospect to feel he or she is more important than anyone else.

Q: Should You Ask a Prospect for Lunch on Your First Telephone Call?

A: If you're coming in from out of town, then possibly. If you're developing a warm rapport on the phone and it seems natural and convenient, then possibly. Generally, though, most decision-makers want to enjoy lunch with those they know. You could come across as brash or lacking in taste to ask on a cold, first-time telephone call.

Q: What About Smoking When Taking a Prospect or Customer to Lunch?

A: Only if the others at the table are smoking. There are strong feelings about smoking and people who smoke. Why risk negative feelings over a few cigarettes? Never smoke in the prospect's office even if he or she is smoking.

Q: What Kind of Entertaining Is Most Productive?

A: Taking both husband and wife out. And as you get to know them better, find ways to include the entire family. When possible take them to someplace unique. The spouse can be a wonderful "influencer." You are building a positive, wholesome identity. Be careful that you and the prospect don't leave others out by talking all business. If it's a prospect, you need to gather the most important information possible. That isn't marketing information; it's personal information. Be sure you jot down the names of the children on your prospect card later.

Q: What About "Doing the Town" with a Prospect or Customer?

A: Don't do it if it's just the two of you. I can just hear the disagreements on this, how it produced some big orders. Certainly it has. But usually a big drinking bout produces some loss of self-respect the following day coupled with guilt. Everything you do with a prospect or customer should help "lift" that person's self-esteem. There should be no guilt trips over personal matters that shouldn't have been discussed or subconscious resentment toward you over feeling awful the next day. Business obtained that way seems to attract problems. And, of course, instead of the spouse being a good influencer, the spouse becomes a resenter.

Hunting trips are a different story. But again, watch the extent of the drinking so there won't be guilt feelings over what was personally disclosed.

Q: How Should a Woman Handle Someone Trying to Get Personally Acquainted?

A: Women have a number of advantages in selling. One is that they may find it easier to get an appointment. Women also have an intuitive advantage. A disadvantage is that a prospect may string them along. The prospect lets them continue to make calls even though there is no intention of considering the product or service. This is quite unfair, but usually a woman senses it. She must remain friendly but businesslike. Dropping a few remarks about her husband or a very special, close friend may get the right message across.

Q: Is it a Good Idea to Give Gifts?

A: Yes, but only if you chalk it up to goodwill and don't try to buy business with it. The gift should not make a person feel obligated or embarrassed. It should not be something that would have to be returned because of a company's policy. Keep in mind that you set a precedent if it's a Christmas gift. Unexpected, unusual gifts that pertain to a person's interests are great. If you think the customer or prospect might worry about what others in the office would think, then don't give it. Unexpected humorous gifts are excellent.

Generally, stay away from the cheap junk with your company's name all over it. In some cases the items are appreciated by employees, but generally the decision-maker isn't impressed. Be careful with Christmas gifts. Slight a few influencers and they won't forget it. Big fruit baskets or gifts for all to share create the warm feelings you want. If you're giving something special to the decision-maker, such as a fruit basket, send it to the home so it can be enjoyed by the whole family. You will win the gratitude of special "influencers."

Q: In Industrial Selling, How Do You Find Out What the Real Specifications Are?

A: Develop a friendly rapport and make inquiries. Try to get a "walk-through" of the plant. You might ask, "Do you have a few minutes? I'd certainly like to have a quick tour of your operation." On the quick tour you will probably pick up information, ideas, and meet others.

Q: When Is it Timely to Bring in Your Sales Manager or Someone Else at Your Company?

A: When you want to play up a "specialist" at your company. When you need an excuse to make another follow-up call. When you can use it as leverage to see your prospect's boss or the screen's boss. Sometimes it's used to build customer goodwill and show that your management cares. It gets management close to in-the-field problems. Perhaps the manager can get insight into the real reasons why you're not getting the business. Sometimes you will bring in another to help close the sale.

If you are a woman and have made an appointment with a male prospect, do not unexpectedly show up with your male manager. Remember the male ego. You'll do better by yourself unless it is understood that you are bringing him along.

Q: How Do You Interrupt a Person Who Talks at Length About Things Other than Business?

A: Even though you say, "Excuse me, but . . . " you're going to bruise the ego. It's hard not to feel foolish when you've gotten carried away and someone wants to change the subject. But there are ways to do it and keep the ego intact. One, of course, is to wait for an opening and jump in. Another is to interrupt with, "Jim, excuse me, but I've got to find a rest room; is it down the hall?" Your talker gives you instructions, interrupting his own line of thought, and usually when you return you can open the conversation as you reenter the room.

However, your very listening to a person's nonbusiness talk may be taking you right into the close. You are fulfilling one of the most crying needs of today: understanding. The ability to listen with concern is one of the greatest assets in selling.

Q: What Visuals Are Best to Use?

A: The best ones are those that show anything dramatically. For example, in chemical refining there are disks installed at various points on the cracking towers. If the pressure gets too high, the disk ruptures, thus avoiding an explosion. Showing an actual ruptured disk gets the message across with more impact than a picture. Find ways to use imaginative showmanship.

Cutaways and blown-up pictures get attention. Slides are good for limited use. The problem with slides is that you lose eye contact with your prospect. The portable overhead is excellent because you can project on a wall or screen and keep full lighting and eye contact as you talk. Keep any visual simple and uncluttered. If your slide presentation is long, interrupt it with lights and talk every eight to ten minutes.

Q: How Long Should You Wait in the Lobby?

A: With an appointment, twenty to twenty-five minutes is ample. Then write on your card, in a friendly way, "Had to get to another appointment. I'll give you a call for best time to get together." You're not trying to make anyone feel guilty, but you do have to maintain respect. And your time is valuable too. People get tied up and may forget you're waiting. So, after about ten minutes, check with the receptionist. As a double check, you might ask to use her phone to talk with the prospect's secretary directly. More than once I've had them say, "Oh, my goodness, Mr. Patton, he must have forgotten you were waiting. Just a moment and I'll check with him."

Q: When Do You Use the First Name?

A: When someone calls you by your first name it is certainly appropriate for you to do the same. However, use your intuition on this. A lot depends on the personality of the individual and also your own type of personality. Acceptance varies with different industries and even parts of the country. For example, people in the ad business call each other by first names within minutes after meeting. People in California and Texas get into first names quickly, while they're more formal in the Northeast.

If you are much younger than the prospect, you may feel more comfortable using the last name for a while even though you are being called by your first name. Frequently, women find it more professional to use the last name for a while. If in doubt and you would feel comfortable calling the person by their first name, ask. A simple, "May I call you John?" does it.

Q: How Do You Hold a Prospect in a Store So They Won't Look Elsewhere?

A: Give them a minute of breathing room to let their senses take in the store. Immediately rushing up as they walk in the door puts some people on the defensive. Then the "May I help you?" usually brings a "No thanks, we're just looking." With that, it's hard to get back with them to build a rapport. On the other hand, a little experience in reading body language tells you when the person is saying, "Here I am, and I need some help."

A better sentence might be a warm and casual, "How can I help you today?" Then if they say they want to look, you can smile and say, "Fine, and I'll be close by if you have any questions." As soon as you read that I've-got-a-question look, you move in quickly. Remember, you hold people by that smile and sincere attitude of wanting to help. Depending upon the type of store, you have to think of reasons to get their names and phone numbers. If they do walk out of your store and you give them a call later, you'll probably be the only store that cared enough. You can frequently get their names by suggesting the idea of putting them on your mailing list. Warm hospitality holds people: "How about a nice, cool Coke while you're looking?"

A neat little area with cookies and coffee, fresh orange juice, or lemonade is a bother, but usually very profitable.

Q: Should You Leave a Brochure When You Feel the Request Is a Way to Get Rid of You?

A: You could say, "May I mail you one? This is the only one I have with me." It gives you a chance to get your name visually in front of the prospect a day or two later. Also, it gives you a reason to make a follow-up phone call with, "Did you get the brochure? You did? Good. I've got something else I wanted to show you. Are you going to be in your office at about 4:15 this afternoon? I need your opinion on something." When you do leave any material be sure your card is stapled to every piece.

Q: How Do You Get Back a Customer Whom Someone Else in Your Company Lost?

A: Try to make an appointment with him or her. And don't expect to get the business back on one call. Be the concerned listener. Do apologize for the company or the misunderstanding or whatever. Try to get the customer to get all of it out of his or her system. Don't sell on this call. You are selling only your warmth and understanding. The person still may not like the company but like you well enough to start ordering again. In some cases a team call with your management is in order, depending on the circumstances.

Q: How Do You Get Back a Customer Whom You Lost?

A: You must have no resentment in you. If you do, it will come through. This can be difficult if it's also the customer's fault. Program your mind on the way to the call, as explained earlier. Try to get into your customer's shoes. Possibly write a short, warm letter of apology. Do not ask for the business back at this point. Follow with a phone call for an appointment. And after you apologize for the mistake, remember, it's yours even if it was the shipping department's fault, hopefully the customer will talk. Again, you are a very concerned listener. If the customer won't talk, wait for a week or so. Also, you owe it to your management to openly discuss it with them so you can plan the best strategy to get the business back.

Q: What Hazards Are There When You Call to Tell the Prospect's Secretary that You'll Be a Few Minutes Late?

A: The prospect could have been on the phone, and the secretary forgot to tell him when he got off. When you walk in to see the prospect, double check. Ask, "Did your secretary get the message to you that I was going to be a few minutes late?"

Q: How Do You Explain the Weaknesses of Your Competition to a Prospect?

A: If your prospect is already using a competitive product or service, you have to be particularly careful not to put him on the defensive. If he made the decision to buy the product or service, then emotionally he may not wish to accept what you're saying. Consider saving face with testimonials here: how certain customers were using the other and now switched to what you're offering. Give the exact reasons the customers gave for switching.

Generally, in selling you don't knock the competition, but there are times when an "analysis" must be done. There are times when you owe your prospect the truth. That would happen when a competitor is being considered and you know the prospect has been misled and is going to make a major mistake.

Suggested method: "Mr. Jeffery, let me put my consulting hat on a moment and compare these two, point for point."

Q: What Do You Do When the Prospect Is Knocking Your Competitor?

A: Listen, perhaps nod a bit. Don't comment too much here. Much better that they do the talking . . . and the knocking. Then, too, there are some buyers who are testing you. Much better to come back with this example: "Yes, I have heard some comments like that. Actually, they put out a fair product in that price range. What our customers seem to like about our product is that it wears so much longer. You don't have down-time problems."

Q: What Do You Do When Someone Is Praising Your Competitor?

A: Listen, nod pleasantly, being careful not to show any bristling. Then comment favorably. "Some companies seem to like it . . . etc." Next go into testimonial anecdotes about why your customers made the change to your company. These do not necessarily have to be stories involving the competitor that your prospect is praising.

Q: How Do You Find Out What Bid Will Probably Get the Business?

A: After you establish rapport with a prospect you can sometimes ask, "Jim, it looks like I'll probably be coming in somewhere around $16,000 to $20,000. Do you think I'm in the ballpark with that?" Listen closely for the inflections, not just the words in the answer.

Q: In Working Up Spec Quotes, How Can You Tell if a Person Is Just Using You?

A: You ask, "Is this for budgeting, or has the money already been allotted?" If it's just for budget figure-gathering, then use your judgment whether you want to spend time on it. The buyer may simply be finding a way to get a figure bracket for a budget proposal to management.

Q: Are There Problems Coming Back with a Lower Bid After You Find Your First One Was Too High?

A: Some buyers resent your coming back with a lower bid. Others welcome it. It depends on the buyer. A way to handle it would be something like: "Jim, I thought we had a good chance on this. We could have made a mistake in figuring the hours. I'd like to refigure it and get right back to you."

Q: What About Leaving Calls . . . or Should You Call Back?

A: Do both. Generally, I like to do the calling back. You may be out if the prospect returns your call or you may be tied up on the phone. If you do ask that the prospect return the call, give your company name along with your name. Some people resent returning a call they think might be important and then getting a sales pitch.

I find it best to leave your name and company name for the prospect and the message that you will be calling back. Leaving your name builds a little curiosity, and your name registers better when you finally get through to the prospect.

Never take it personally if a prospect doesn't return your calls. Some very busy people find ten to twenty messages when they get back to the office. As the seller, yours isn't priority.

Q: On the Phone, How Can You Sense Whether Your Timing Is Good or Bad?

A: Your prospect may have your competitor or his boss sitting right there. Notice any clipped words or guarded answers, or a flat voice. Ask, "Are you up to your ears or am I possibly interrupting a meeting?" It gives him an out. He may tell you that he's pretty busy right now. Suggest calling him later or the next day.

Q: How Do You Keep from Losing Out to Low-price Quotes in a Sealed Bid?

A: By the time you get a request to quote, you're probably too late. This is why it's so valuable to develop in-depth rapport with a number of people in a company that you're calling on. The project engineer can tell you about something they're planning for early next year. Then he tells you the "specs" haven't been written yet. In the conversation you find out exactly who will be writing them. If possible, try to influence this person to specify certain features. If your product is the only one with such features, you have an excellent advantage if this is written into the specs.

Let's suppose a number of companies can provide what you do. Then you definitely must develop a good rapport prior to the date when the requests for bids go out. In many cases the request for bids is simply a formality. The person who will get the business frequently has been working closely with various departments for some time.

16

Getting Rid of Stupid Habits

*A*ny habit that hurts you physically or mentally in your enjoyment of life is stupid. Probably 98 percent of everything we do is habit. Certainly, most habits serve us well. But there are a handful that are downright unhealthy . . . and therefore stupid to continue. This chapter will show you how to get rid of them.

Smoking probably heads the list of stupid habits. Take your pick in the order of the next four: Toxic thinking, overeating, not wearing a seat belt, and drinking too much.

We're all vulnerable to these habits, but salespeople are particularly so with their stressful life-styles and restless temperament. The pressures on salespeople are constant. They must produce. Their efforts are closely tracked by computers, allowing no letting up in trying for a high sales call to closing ratios.

Let's look at the smoking habit. The nicotine of smoking relieves stress momentarily by triggering a rise in the blood sugar, which gives a person a bit of a lift. Then the immediate rise in blood sugar, in turn, triggers insulin into the bloodstream from the pancreas, producing a new low and tension. That brings on an emotional urge for another cigarette.

What about overeating? The pleasure of eating was programmed into us early. As adults, stress and frustrations can bring on cravings for relief by eating something. Since selling is a people business, salespeople are subjected to another cause of overeating. In the course of business and entertaining customers, salespeople are frequently subjected to the full-course meal with heavy sauces and trappings of "gourmet junk food."

What about the stupid habit of not using a seat belt? The restless, impatient nature of many salespeople goes against the grain of snapping on the seat belt, even though wearing a seat belt is law in many states. Add to that their optimistic "everything's going to be okay" unconcern.

How does one, realistically, get rid of one or more of these habits? We're going to cover them one at a time. First, let's identify a habit. Exciting new brain research is unveiling how habits are formed and stay in place. Experiments with rats and monkeys by Georges Ungar at the Baylor College of Medicine indicate that there is probably a different protein or amino acid molecular structure for each and every learned skill we have. A habit is a learned skill. Each new habit you learn has its own specific chemical neurotransmitter firing from neuron to neuron.

Here are the reactions that are probably going on in your brain as you replace one habit with another. Packed between your brain's billions of neurons are about 100 billion glia cells. These glia cells nourish the neuron cell with oxygen and other substances so that they may make special protein combinations. These strings of protein molecules go down the stem of the neuron axis to the firing position at the synapse gap. When the new skill habit is started a new type of protein molecule is formed by the neurons and fired across the gaps to dendrite receptors of other neurons.

Evidence shows that a skill is formed by a constant flow of these new neurotransmitters across the gaps. Like keys fitting specific locks, these new protein neurotransmitters must fit into certain receptors. This chain goes on through millions, possibly billions, of neurons. It takes a bit of time for the new chemical neurotransmitters to be formed. Thus, it is thought, when we learn any skill we need both time and repetition to let this network become established in the brain.

To get rid of a stupid habit you must learn a new skill. In this case the new skill will take the place of the old. A physical example would be changing your stroke in tennis to hit through the ball. It must be programmed into the brain. Logical desire won't do it; There must be emotional desire. You might see the logic in hitting through the ball, but that probably would not cause much stir in the brain cells. Emotionally, if you wanted *to look good to others* on the court or raise your level of play to be acceptable on court *with certain people* or *beat* a certain person, changes in the brain would take place. The new habit patterns of hitting through the ball would start forming.

If you've got one of the five stupid habits, let's go after it. You can't use forces of influence and persuasion very well if you're sickly, half alive, or dead. If you've got several of these habits, don't take them on all at once. It won't work. Change them one at a time.

Changing "toxic thinking" was covered in the chapter "Programming Your Mind" and the chapter "Toxic Thinking." You may want to reread those chapters.

SMOKING

Three hundred twenty-four thousand Americans die prematurely each year from smoking. That would be comparable to seven commercial air crashes a day. One air crash is spread all over TV, newspapers, and magazines; it's front-page stuff. Not so with the deadly figure from smoking. The facts from the American Medical Association, the government, and the American Cancer Society are real and substantiated.

Ninety percent of all lung cancer is a direct result of smoking. Emphysema kills many thousands every year and leaves many more thousands clinging to life, miserably gasping or keeping an oxygen bottle nearby.

Why do so many intelligent people smoke? Because they emotionally want to. They've read the facts. They know that it not only can, but probably will, cause cancer. They know it's dumb to smoke. It's not macho. It's not smart. It's not sophisticated. But we humans are emotional animals. Probably 85 percent of everything we do is emotional. When it comes to a decision between logic and emotion the emotional reason will almost always win out. We frequently do something emotional and then tack on a so-called logical reason to justify it. How often have you heard: "Trouble is, if I quit smoking, I might gain weight."

One of my good friends had everything. He was bright. He built a fine business. He made enough money to build a beautiful home on a thirty-three-acre hilltop, and had his own sailboat in the Caribbean. He was an excellent salesman, but he worried a lot and had an impatient temperament. Cigarettes were his most comforting companions. I was there when they told him his lungs and liver were too far gone to even operate. Logically, he knew he should have quit. But emotionally he didn't want to. He had the cigarette *Mind Set*. That Mind Set overcame the logical thinking.

If someone you care about smokes, ask him or her to read this chapter. If you smoke, you must quit, and quit now. But to quit you must emotionally—not logically—want to. You can absolutely quit smoking right now by changing your emotional *Mind Set*. When I say quit right now I'm talking about the next few minutes, after you are through reading this! I'm going to carry you through the process of quitting. It's not easy, I know. I smoked two and a half packs a day for years. I quit by changing my emotional Mind Set.

As a smoker, let's start with what's going on in your brain. You were beautifully "programmed" somewhere in childhood or your teens that smoking was macho and sophisticated. Maybe you didn't start that early, but billboards, movies, and observing young, vigorous people smoking made an impression. You tried it. Strong neuron connections were made. Make no mistake, millions of very real neurons were setting up very real physical connections between new neurotransmitters and new dendrite receptors. You now had a new Mind Set for smoking.

When you felt uneasy or shy at a party a cigarette felt good. More reinforcement of millions of neuron connections that plugged into shyness or uneasiness. It was enjoyable with coffee or after sex. More connections. The habit was in place. Automatically, you reached for a cigarette when there was any stress.

As explained above, stress is relieved because nicotine raises the blood sugar. The blood sugar "high" falls to a lower point than it was previously. The neurons flash the message that a lift is needed. Automatically, without your really being aware of it, the hand goes to the cigarette pack. It's a vicious cycle.

Smoking doesn't just kill. Smoking severely cuts memory recall. It cuts the oxygen to your brain. The damage cuts your vision, your skin looks older, you age prematurely, your voice changes. Smoking raises the blood pressure and is one of the primary causes of heart attacks.

Your clothes smell, and so does your breath. The odor clings to your office, home, and car. You can't stay in top physical shape. Each cigarette cuts out 25 milligrams of Vitamin C in your body. Colds and bronchitis come more often. Then there's the mess, the ashtrays, the burned holes, the smelly fingers, and the expense. However, the cost of the tobacco is small compared to what you'll end up paying in medical expenses.

You can and must change all that right now. We're going down into Deep Alpha where your brain cycles are about ten per second. At this relaxed level you can best program your brain with a new network of neuron connections, a new habit.

You will change the smoking habit to a nonsmoking habit. You may have already tried to quit by using logic and discovered how difficult that is. So we've got to "motivate" new neuron connections. The only way is through emotion and intense interest. Something about not smoking has got to turn you on right now.

Here are a few reasons that may move you. Go through them. If just one of them moves you emotionally, you will have a new neurotransmitter chemical, a newly formed molecule chain, making connections. The fight for the takeover of these new neurotransmitters at millions of synapse gaps in your brain will go on for two to five weeks. It will be a tough battle at those gaps, but you can do it with *emotion*. As you read the following, which hits you *emotionally?*

1. If you're not coughing now, you will. The air enters your lungs through the bronchi tubes. These tubes are lined with millions of tiny hairs called cilia. They vibrate back and forth 900 times a minute. Their job is to keep the solid pollutants in the air from entering the lungs. With continual smoking, they no longer stand up and vibrate. They bend over and quit, lie down, or disappear from the lining of the bronchi. The body, in an effort to block the impurities, rushes in a flow of mucus to the barren areas. The mucus is trying to do the cilia's job of trapping pollutants. But the mucus itself builds up and gets trapped in the bronchi. You cough to release the mucus. Finally, your "smokers cough" becomes so regular you're hardly aware of it. Cancerous lesions form under the mucus. Once started, the cell growth is rapid, spreading to the lung tissue, and then through the lymphatic system to other organs.

2. When the elastic of your undershorts goes they droop and fall off. There's nothing you can do about it.

   Smoking causes the same thing to happen to the elasticity of your lungs. That elasticity of bringing air in gets saggy. It is destroyed cigarette by cigarette. Like your undershorts, once the elasticity is destroyed, it will never return. It happens very gradually . . . just a little with every cigarette.

   In the early stages you don't think much about it unless you do some running. Over time it gets worse. You can't get the oxygen you want. You're not aware of the fact that some of the air sacs in your lungs are bursting and collapsing. It gets tougher to get your breath. You have the first stages of emphysema. This can happen to you while you're still quite young. But you probably won't die for some time. You'll drag around for years, huffing, mouth open, tired, and coughing.

3. If the prospects of even mild emphysema don't emotionally phase you, how about looking old before your time? You say, "But I look good. I'm thirty-two years old and I'm active. I'm attractive." Ten years go by so fast. In those few years smoking will age that skin twenty years. It will dry prematurely due to constriction of the blood capillaries. Lots of small lines in the face begin to form before they should. Each cigarette you put in your mouth is aging you. Your eyes are not as bright as they would have been without smoking; also, they are not as fully open and expressive and attractive. They get a slitlike appearance.

   Your teeth look older. Brightness is gone. Perhaps they're slightly discolored from the nicotine. Your voice sounds older, gets an unpleasant raspiness or harshness. And you're not very attractive as you punch a dirty cigarette out in an ashtray. Your clothes smell, and some people don't want you around. They've read how an entire room is contaminated for twelve minutes following just one cigarette. And who likes to see dropped ashes on the floor or table?

4. Suppose a doctor told you right now that you had to have a brain operation. Suppose he said you'd be okay except that you'd lose 10 to 23 percent of your ability to remember. That's what smoking does to your brain. You see, your brain uses 25 percent of your body's total intake of oxygen, yet your brain is approximately 3 percent of your total weight. Smoking cuts the oxygen supply to the brain by 50 percent. Your vision is cut by one-fifth. But you probably don't miss it. The same is true of your sense of smell. It's no longer sharp. You've gotten used to it.

5. What about your efficiency? A number of employers are aware of mental limitations that result from smoking. However, most are more concerned about how smoking steals away productive time. Studies show this can amount to five minutes an hour, added up in seconds looking for a cigarette, finding a match, lighting it, dragging on it, looking for an ashtray. The time wasted comes to twenty-three working days a year! And that's not counting the proneness to colds and time off.

If I've made you angry with some of these facts, go check their validity. They shocked me too. Maybe you're thinking, "We all gotta go sometime." Right. But the effects of smoking can make you look old and feel half alive for many years before you actually die. That doesn't seem like much fun.

Hopefully, one of the above has grabbed you hard enough so that right now you emotionally want to quit smoking. If so, great! The following suggestions will help you "kick the habit."

Put this book down, get up, and physically change something in the room. Leave it in it's new place for five weeks. Put a lamp on a different table or a glass turned upside down in a conspicuous place. Put a wastebasket in a different spot. You want to be constantly reminded of your decision. You're using a present neuron pattern to constantly reinforce your new neuron pattern. Take every ashtray and put it out of sight. Put the cigarettes you have in the toilet right now. Watch the awful brown color that comes off them in the water.

You have just made a major decision in your life! It is truly one of your finest decisions. To make it stick, let's go into Deep Alpha and program the new Mind Set. Take yourself down to Alpha 10 much as you did in the second chapter. First, read the following steps taking you down to Alpha and the suggested affirmations. Then put those steps and affirmations in your own words. You can do this out loud or silently, as you wish. Get comfortable, but don't lie down. You don't want to go to sleep. Also, you don't want to be disturbed. Possibly the only way to get away from people and telephones is to go somewhere in the car and park. If so, do it.

Then say to yourself: "I no longer desire to smoke. I am now going down into Deep Alpha and I am programming into the neurons of my brain the fact that I am no longer a smoker. I am now very relaxed. My entire body is relaxed. All the tension is going out of my face, out of my neck . . . out of my arms . . . and out of my fingertips. All the tension is going out of my legs . . . completely . . . and on out of my toes. Nineteen . . . eighteen . . . deeper . . . deeper . . . seventeen . . . sixteen . . . deeper . . . deeper . . . fifteen . . . fourteen . . . I am now getting into Deep Alpha. Let go . . . let go . . . let go. I am completely relaxed. Thirteen . . . deeper . . . deeper . . . My body is completely relaxed. Twelve . . . deeper . . . deeper . . . deeper . . . eleven . . . ten.

"I am now in Deep Alpha. I am programming my mind and my body. I no longer am a smoker. I no longer want a cigarette. Cigarettes smell. They make my fingers smell. I feel sorry for people who smoke. They are chained to a stupid habit. If I get the urge to smoke, I will wait a few minutes and think what a cigarette does to my brain, my skin, my eyes, and my lungs. I am strong. I am sending strong messages in my brain that I am no longer a smoker. I now will see better, remember better, taste better, smell better. I am a clean, bright person. I am more attractive and healthier in every way.

"Other people smoking does not bother me. I feel sorry for them. I will try to help them quit. I accept this. It is now programmed."

Now either open your eyes or count back up from ten to twenty and then open your eyes. Go into Deep Alpha like this each and every day for five weeks. For the next few days you might read the countdown to Alpha first before putting it in your own words. Do not try to program in other affirmations or try to change any other habit for the five weeks. This is too important. It deserves your total concentration until the new neuron patterns are set.

In addition to changing something in the room, put some odd thing in your pocket or purse as a constant reminder that you are no longer a smoker. As you touch the object or notice the object you have moved in the room, quietly make this affirmation: "I am more attractive and healthier than ever. . . . I am no longer a smoker. I accept this . . . it is now programmed." As you say this, press your thigh with your finger. You are involving millions more neuron connections with this touch.

Also, put something weird in your car for five weeks. This could be something as simple as a Band-Aid on the dash. Whatever it is, it must be where you will notice it. It is another constant reminder that you are a nonsmoker. You no longer want to smoke. Each time you notice this weird, out-of-place object say the affirmations above. Each time close with: "I accept this . . . it is now programmed." You want all areas where you spend time to have something you will notice: work, home, car, on your person. And don't be lazy about the affirmations. Say them each time you're reminded. Constantly saying those affirmations is very important, along with the daily meditation into Deep Alpha.

The neurons are now getting new messages, reinforced by sight of the out-of-place objects and by touch. The new neurotransmitters are being fired across the gaps to other neurons. On occasions such as having coffee or a drink, or when you are having a bit of an emotional upheaval over something, the neurons will start firing those old neurotransmitters. Those old patterns have been formed over a long time. You'll experience this as an urge and a feeling of "To heck with it. . . . I've got to have a cigarette." Meet it by touching your thigh with your finger and saying, "I am in control. I am a nonsmoker. I am getting brighter, healthier, and more attractive day by day. I am happy about this. I accept this . . . it is now programmed."

Let your friends who don't smoke know you have quit. Their support helps. Also, you may be a bit irritable for a while. They'll understand. And quit cold. No tapering off. No empty holder in the mouth. You've broken the chain. You are your own person!

Emotional events and stress can suddenly send you after a pack of cigarettes. The chances are about fifty-fifty that you will backslide. Here and there some battles at the synapse gaps may be lost. Don't get the guilties, please. Toss the things in the toilet as soon as you get hold of your resolve. Then go into Deep Alpha and begin again. If it happens again, just do the same.

You will no longer be a smoker. You will feel a new pride. Welcome to a great new life . . . without cigarettes!

OVEREATING

Stress frequently seeks relief in eating. Eating is emotional enjoyment. We were programmed to it as babies. It feels good. The patterns in those brain neurons for oral gratification started early. The pleasurable, comfortable experience has been well charted in our minds. Therefore, it gives us immediate relief from frustration, loneliness, and emotional and stressful situations.

Worse, we're constantly bombarded with stimuli to eat. Pictures of food are everywhere . . . TV, billboards, magazines. Restaurants, fast-food places, ice cream parlors line the main streets. Food and drink is the theme of most social get-togethers.

The salesperson is particularly subjected to food and drink in entertaining. Frequently, it's the multicourse, high-caloric meal. Eating alone in hotels, the salesperson has a hard time getting ample fresh fruit or vegetables that haven't been drained of vitamins through over cooking.

No one wants to be fat. No one starts out to be fat. Those programmed messages in the brain constantly tell us to put food into our mouths. It gives us pleasurable relief from frustrations, boredom, and stress.

Then we notice we've put just a few pounds on the stomach, thighs, or hips. That bothers us with a gnawing dissatisfaction. We want emotional relief from that feeling. We get it in the immediate pleasure of eating something more. It's a tough cycle to break.

Before long, we're a little overweight and have to do something about it. So we'll do spurts of exercising, then undo it all with a few bouts of eating. One day, in a bit of self-disgust, we look at ourselves in a group snapshot someone took. We're not just a bit overweight, we're fat. Maybe we get on one of those quick-weight-loss programs. It works for a while. We take off some pounds. But the craving is still there. Stresses of life continue. Six months later we're back up again.

The key is to change the habit. Overeating is a stupid habit. In selling, you must keep up a good appearance, be highly active, stay in trim shape with high energy. You can reverse the weight problem by reversing the influencers in your brain. You must reprogram that brain. The messages of "feel good with more food" must be changed to "feel good with less food."

You can do it. You can start that reversal right this moment as you're reading this. It won't be through an agonizing diet or calorie counting. Instead, you will change the messages in the control center, your brain. But to do this you must have a strong *emotional* desire that will take the place of the "feel good" desire of putting something in your mouth.

Find that emotional desire right now by going over the following eight things about overeating. As you read them, which one moves you *emotionally*?

1. "If I lost weight I'd look great in that jacket (or dress)." This may be one that you've looked at, seen in a catalog, or seen someone wear.
2. "I'd look great in jeans if I didn't have those pounds on my stomach."
3. "So and so would really go for me if I were trim." So and so should be a real person.
4. "I'd like to look more athletic, with a flat, hard stomach."
5. "I hate looking like this. It makes me look older than I am."
6. "To move up in my career I've got to look good. The new breed

of executives are taking care of themselves. They're getting exercise, watching their eating, and staying trim."

7. "I'd look and feel great at the pool or playing tennis or dancing if I lost weight."
8. "I don't want to end up with high blood pressure, a heart attack, diabetes, or cancer." The National Health and Nutrition Study and the American Cancer Society's studies show that these diseases are greatly increased in overweight people.

Did you feel an emotional tug when you read one of those? If you did, you're ready to reprogram your brain to a new you.

What you're going to do is lose fat. You will look and feel great. And you will certainly be healthier.

From one of those eight "pictures" above you must have felt an emotional tug, or pull, or sinking feeling. If not, you're not ready to lose weight. You're going to ride that emotion you just felt. It's your big friend. It's going to change those neuron connections in your brain. Latch on to it. Paint that emotional picture in more detail. Put in people, the ones you care about and from whom you want caring and admiring reactions. Put in how you'll look as you catch your reflection from a storefront glass. Add certain kinds of clothes you'll wear, including the colors. Picture the places you'll go, and the people who will see you.

Hang on to that picture now. Try to "feel" the fact that your new, trim look influences people favorably. At this very moment, that "picturing" and that "feeling," even if hazy, are causing millions of new neuron connections to form in your brain. It's the beginning. Oh, there will be a big battle at the synaptic gaps in your brain. It's already started. Certain neuron transmitters don't want to be outmaneuvered by new ones. It wasn't very hard on them with just plain dieting. They still maintained their old connections of deep desire to put food in the mouth.

And don't get the guilties if you compulsively finish off a box of cookies or order a hot fudge sundae. You're going to lose a few battles on the way, but you'll win the war. That "picture" you're holding is establishing new connections. These will be reinforced with other mental programming. You'll lose weight, very definitely. To do it you'll be going down into Deep Alpha at least once a day, just as explained in chapter 2. This will be your primary programming until you hit the weight you're after.

You can, if you wish, program in other affirmations such as

boldness and confidence, higher income, and so on. But your mind must know that the big goal is that you no longer overeat. Do not attempt to quit the smoking habit at the same time. It also must get primary concentration.

Let's go, right now, into Deep Alpha. Read the following first. Then put it all in your own words. Do this every day until you reach the goal you want. If you want to take off twenty or thirty pounds, start with a goal of ten pounds. Be realistic about this goal. You came into this world with certain genetic DNA programming. So your heritage has an influence on your bone structure. What we're after is unnecessary flab and fat.

Here we go: the big start. You are going to literally form new neurotransmitters that set up new patterns in your brain that will change your eating habits and your weight. You are headed for wonderful, exciting results. Get very comfortable. Do not lie down, or you may go to sleep. However, do not be concerned should you doze a bit in any of your daily sessions. It may happen from time to time. But you're not after a quick energy nap here. Be sure nothing will disturb you. Unplug the phone.

Say something like this, silently or out loud, as you wish: "I am now going into Deep Alpha. I am going to program my mind and my body. My body is getting slimmer and slimmer every day in every way. I am very relaxed now. All the tension is going out of my neck, my shoulders, my face, and my arms . . . right on out of my fingertips. I am very relaxed." Now take yourself down to Deep Alpha, as you did in chapter 2. Count from nineteen to Alpha 10.

After you get to ten let a minute or two go by as you wait for thoughts to drift out of your mind, but don't be concerned with them. You are trying for complete stillness physically and mentally. Now begin the affirmations.

"My body is getting slimmer and slimmer every day in every way. Today I am losing three ounces."

Next, affirm something about that "emotional feeling" that you just had. For example, you are looking more attractive to such and such a person. Use the "picture" or "feeling" that hit you.

Now go into another affirmation: "Half is better than all. Half is better than all. Half is better than all. Today I will eat half instead of all. I will leave food on my plate. Today I am losing three ounces. My body is getting slimmer and slimmer every day in every way."

I can hear someone saying, "Just three ounces a day!"

Right. And that's about four pounds every three weeks. That's fast enough to let your metabolism adjust. Forget the fast pound-a-day hype you see in the ads. If you have any questions regarding your weight or this method, check with your doctor. Another reason for the three ounces a day is your subconscious mind. It must "buy" your idea, or the new neuron connections won't be reinforced. The subconscious must "believe it." It can "believe" three ounces a day. Remember, your mind has been thoroughly programmed to the weight you are right now. It is getting a new Mind Set because it is believable. What's more, you're not having to go through an agonizing diet. Oh, you're going to watch what you put in your mouth. But, it won't be steely willpower. It will be because you are "programmed" to the right foods.

Program in right eating with these affirmations: "I like healthy foods. I am repulsed by junk food and fattening food. I love to nibble on crisp raw vegetables. I look great and feel great. I am my own person. I have no problem ordering just soup and salad if that's what I really want. I am getting slimmer and slimmer every day in every way."

Next, program in excercise: "I look for ways to exercise every day. As I walk or run, I fill my lungs with oxygen. My mind clears. I get intuitive insights. Afterward I am relaxed. I think better. I feel better. I like myself better. I have high energy. I look great and feel great."

End with something like this: "I am getting slimmer and slimmer every day in every way. I am getting more attractive every day. I accept this. It is now programmed into millions of neurons in my brain. When I go back to the Beta level [brainwaves about twenty cycles per second] I will be refreshed and feel great."

You may open your eyes or you may choose to count your way up . . . ten, eleven, and so on to twenty. Be certain you are going into Deep Alpha at least once a day.

Also, as with the smoking habit, use various objects to remind you of your program throughout the day. Put anything crazy or unusual in your purse or pocket, a large safety pin, perhaps. Change something at home in the room where you spend the most time; for example, put a tumbler upside down on the mantle. Stick something odd on the wheel or dashboard of your car, perhaps a mailing label. Change something physical at work such as moving a wastebasket.

Throughout the day, as these out-of-place things are noticed, go *immediately* into an affirmation such as: "I am getting slimmer and slimmer every day in every way. I am losing three ounces today." Then think a thought about your own emotional "feeling." At the same time, touch your thigh with your finger. You will now be adding the sense of touch. That means millions and millions more neurons are linked up and reinforcing your new pattern, and it will be happening over and over again every day. Don't pass this off as silly; please do it. Do it quickly each and every time you notice one of the objects. The new neurotransmitters are overriding the old neuron patterns that caused the overeating.

A few suggestions: Stay away from full meals. Try to eat slower. Be extra careful in the grocery store. Don't tempt yourself with boxes of cookies and crackers. Move in to the produce department to find appealing things to munch on. Most of us were taught to clean our plates. You will be programming this out and enjoy watching much of it still on your plate when you're through with your meal.

When tempted by fattening foods, at that moment of decision, press yourself on the thigh with a finger and silently make an affirmation such as: "Each day, in every way, I am getting slimmer and slimmer . . . and more attractive in every way." Or, "I am getting more attractive in every way . . . today I am losing three ounces."

Again, if you give in to one of the "battles" now and then, try not to chastise yourself. There's nothing worse than the guilties. Try to put it out of your mind and keep going with the program.

Two months from this date you will weigh ten pounds less. And you'll do it the right way . . . creating a new Mind Set about eating. The beauty is it will stay with you. You won't have the ever-present nagging fight with dieting and calorie counting. You have pro-grammed your mind to eat right.

After that ten pounds go for the next ten if you are still over-weight, and the next ten if that is necessary. But, at this moment, make the first move by getting those objects in place where they'll be noticed.

OVERDRINKING

Salespeople are probably subjected to more drinking than any other group. It's a people business that goes beyond nine to five. Sales-people are entertaining, getting together at conferences, having business lunches, getting together with prospects and customers for after-hours meetings and dinners. Drinking is always present.

Whether you want to or not, you find yourself with a drink in your hand. And if there's uneasiness about making small talk, acting relaxed, feeling more confident, the drink takes care of it. It feels good. And so it goes, over and over again. The relief of stress by having a few drinks is programmed neuron to neuron. The habit becomes set.

One drink makes it easy to order another. The habit transfers from business to social get-togethers, to a regular routine each evening. There is no line between overdrinking and alcoholism. It's a gray area. Alcoholics are already there long before they will admit to the disease.

If you feel you can't control your drinking, it is probably causing real problems right now with your family, job, friends, or health. Try to admit that possibility and make a call to Alcoholics Anonymous. Please do it. You will meet wonderful people. They'll help you lick the problem. Each one in AA has been through it all and suffered greatly. Many of our top salespeople, bright, creative geniuses, and entertainers, belong to AA. Just get to one of their meetings and get to know them.

It would be presumptuous in this book to suggest a different path when the results of joining AA have proved so beneficial. What we're dealing with in this chapter is so-called social and business drinking that's frequently overdone, makes you sick, gives you hangovers, gets you into automobile accidents, dulls your senses each evening.

According to the National Safety Council, 25,000 people die each year in accidents due to alcohol, 650,000 people a year are injured, and 1.5 million are arrested for driving under the influence. It is a grisly tragedy. Overdrinking breaks up families and careers. It breaks a person's health and ages people prematurely. Every drink kills neuron brain cells. It has been well known that alcoholism causes brain deterioration. Lesley A. Cala's research group at the Queen Elizabeth II Medical Centre, using the CAT scan method, has found brain damage in 85 percent of even moderate drinkers. Neuron cells cannot reproduce themselves. Sure, you have billions of cells, but why compromise your sharp mental faculties with a sustained loss by overdrinking?

If you do drink, do so in moderation. This habit is a dangerous kettle of fish. To change it there must be an emotional desire to change. To find out if you feel emotional enough to make the change, see if any of the following fit you or give you an uneasy feeling:

1. You want and feel a need for a drink or two as soon as you get home. This bothers you because some evenings you would really like a clear head for some serious reading.
2. You drink too much now and then and feel like the devil all the next day. The wasted day wasn't worth the night before. Sometimes you're not as sharp as you could be during a sales presentation due to a few too many the night before.
3. You had too much and got sick.
4. You had too much and said and did things you regret. It really hurts when it involves a spouse, children, boss, close friend, or customer.
5. You drove, and you're lucky you didn't hit someone.
6. You drove and did hit someone.
7. Your sex drive is diminishing. Overdrinking does cause this.
8. Your face is getting a dissipated or a puffy look.

If one of the above moves or fits you, let's go into Deep Alpha and change the cause of overdrinking. Let's reprogram those neuron connections with different neurotransmitters. You can do it. You can do it and still drink. But no longer will you make a fool of yourself, wake up with regrets, or feel sick all the next day. You won't muddy up some sales call. You'll always be sharp for meetings. Puffiness will disappear.

You're going to get rid of a very stupid habit—overdrinking. Make the trip to Deep Alpha each day. Use the method, and countdown as in chapter 2. When you get down to Alpha 10, take a few minutes to let your thoughts drift out. Try to quiet yourself physically and mentally. You want no interruptions, no ringing phones. And no drink before going into Alpha.

When you're in Alpha make affirmations closely allied to the point above that caught you emotionally. Put the following in your own words: "I am now in Deep Alpha. I am now going to program my mind and my body. I am completely free of any alcoholic habit. I can take it or leave it. Repeat. I can take it or leave it . . . anytime, anywhere . . . regardless of the situation. I do not have to have a drink. I am my own person. I can easily turn a drink down regardless of who is pushing me to have one. They aren't doing me a favor. I can take it or leave it.

"It is a toxic poison, and I don't like it in my body. One drink is my limit. Half a drink is better. I don't have to have a drink because others do. I am my own person. I do not need a drink to make small talk. I am in control at all times. I'm bright, alert, feel good, and look good. I have guts. I have self-esteem. I can take a drink or leave it . . . anytime, anyplace, no matter who I'm with. I accept this . . . it is now programmed into millions of neurons in my mind."

Program this in daily. Use your own words. Now put some reminders around as described previously in overeating and smoking. Do this for five weeks. In that time you will have reprogrammed the patterns in your brain with new neurotransmitter chemicals. Each time you notice one of the weird objects you've put in place touch your thigh with your finger and say something like the following to reinforce the new traces in your brain:

"I have no problem with not drinking anything alcoholic. I am my own person and can easily turn it down. If I do drink, one is my limit. I am fun, bright, healthy, attractive, with high self-esteem."

When tempted to take a second drink touch your thigh with your finger immediately and pause before you accept. Touching in this way reinforces the millions of neuron connections. Do the same now and then when you get home to pass having a drink each and every evening. You don't want 6:00 P.M. to signal it's time to drink. You are your own person. You can take it or leave it. If you backslide, get right back into the program for five weeks.

NOT WEARING SEAT BELTS

You may be wondering how this could be included with such really important concerns as smoking, being overweight, or drinking too much.

It belongs. It belongs because salespeople in particular are in a car a great deal of the time. Yet, as a group, salespeople don't take the seat belt seriously enough. Forty-five- to fifty-thousand people are killed each year in automobile accidents in the United States, according to the Highway Traffic Safety Administration. Every year 1 million people wouldn't suffer crushed bones and smashed faces if they would just snap on their seat belts.

Slamming into the windshield at 30 mph carries the same force as jumping headfirst out of a third-story window. Forget bracing yourself. Trying to brace yourself in a crash of just 10 mph would be like catching a two-hundred-pound sack dropped from two stories up.

On the street today, one in ten drivers has had so much to drink that his or her driving is seriously impaired. That's every tenth car! Add to that many who are on drugs or people who are just not paying attention. These people are coming at you in the other lane, pulling up to stop signs as you pass by, or trying to pass you.

You may be an excellent driver. But what about the others around you, those you have no control over? Do you realize that statistically you will be in at least one accident every five years? And it could very well be some person out of control who slams into you. With your seat belt on, your chances of coming out of it without serious injury skyrocket. So, for goodness sake, buckle up and be ready for it. You have no idea where or when it will happen. It could be that four-block drive to the store tomorrow. Seventy-five percent of accidents are within twenty-five miles of home.

In retrospect, it's hard for me to believe I had so much trouble with this habit. I got through the smoking one okay after a few backslides. But seat belts? I didn't take them seriously. This is common with people in sales. We're a restless breed, can't be bothered with such particular things as seat belts. I knew the logic. But to change a habit I had to get some emotion into it.

The possibility of losing an eye by going through the windshield was my "emotional turn-on." How stupid I'd feel as I lay in the hospital. The statistic that I will be in at least one accident in the next five years, and at least one serious accident in my life, capped it. I now go for the seat belt. I'm ready for that accident. That's not being pessimistic—just realistic.

Once you decide always to buckle up you'll find it simple to program. Go into Deep Alpha as explained previously. Make the affirmation in your own words, something like this: "I am now going to program my mind. Each time I get into an automobile I immediately look for the seat belt . . . bring it around and snap it. I now see myself doing this. I now hear it snap. I always buckle up. I am prepared for some idiot hitting me. I accept this . . . it is now programmed into millions of neurons in my brain."

You may need a week or two for the neurotransmitters to change in this new habit you have programmed. When the habit is locked in you can eliminate the programming and devote the meditative time to something else.

Those are the big five . . . the really stupid habits that can kill or completely spoil your happiness in life. So take them on . . . one at a time. The devastating drug habit would certainly benefit from mind programming. However, the difficulties of breaking that habit would probably best be handled by personal medical or psychological assistance.

Other habits such as nail-biting, messiness, or being disorganized can be pushed out of the brain with mind programming. They won't kill you, but they can be annoying.

In the next chapter we're going to talk about thirteen pesky habits in selling that can really steal you blind.

17

Thirteen Devils
that Steal

*T*hese habits won't kill you, but they'll slice right into your income. They'll block a salesperson's rise in a company. We all indulge in some of these from time to time; that's human. What you want to look for is that one habit in the group of thirteen that you do regularly. That devil is probably costing you lots of money!

Program that devil habit right out of your brain. Program the positive in Deep Alpha. An example would be if you have a habit of doing paperwork during top selling hours. Program: "I use prime selling time for selling. I do paperwork only at other times." Visualize a clock. Then see yourself catching up on paperwork at 5:00 or 6:00 P.M. Then say, "I accept this . . . it is now programmed."

This daily affirmation should take hold in about three to four weeks. Like any other affirmation, there has to be strong emotional desire or expectancy. So look over the following group. If any fit, get rid of them. The emotional trigger should be that they're really holding you back or putting a lid on your income.

PROCRASTINATION

Pete Putoff had a time with this devil. He called on electrical contractors in the Anaheim area, but he put off getting proposals out. He was always late with sales reports and had an edgy relationship with his manager. He got a real shocker when a large annual order went to a competitor. The contractor told him he would have gotten it, but he put off getting the proposal to him until it was too late.

NO PLANNING

Fran Flighty called on camera stores in Chicago. Her planning was all last minute. She would start planning the day at 9:00 A.M. Frequently, she would crisscross her territory during the day, responding to any request, regardless of urgency or priority. She used up most of her selling time in travel. Rarely did she pay attention to the time she was devoting to small-potential accounts versus high-potential accounts. They had to let Fran go. Actually, she put in the hours . . . but it was all wheel spinning.

AVOIDING POSSIBLE REJECTION

Shakey Reed sold a line of auto parts to auto supply stores in New Jersey and part of Pennsylvania. He couldn't stand rejection so he made as few cold calls as possible. Shakey was always afraid of offending someone. He worried about making a buyer angry if he called back too soon. He was afraid to press for an appointment with the real decision-makers. He was part of the statistic that 64 percent of sales calls are made on the wrong person. Shakey wanted to be liked more than anything. He thought selling was some kind of popularity contest. There was always a nervous smile for anyone who was around. He would accept any objection as understandable. He rarely asked for the order.

NO PERSISTENCE

Karen Quitsoon covered the Southeast United States for a high-tech magazine. She called on both media buyers at ad agencies and advertisers. Karen rarely made two or three callbacks if they said they were happy with their present media selection. She wasn't aware that 80 percent of sales are made after the fifth callback, although 80 percent of salespeople quit after two or three callbacks. That fact turned her around, and now she hangs in there if it's a high-potential account. Because she has a large area some of those callbacks have to be by phone. And she constantly intersperses her calls with notes and other mailings to stay in touch. She rapidly moved from the bottom quarter to the top quarter in total sales.

POOR CALL PREPARATION

Willie Wingit had a big smile. He had a way of getting in to see the heads of large companies. Willie's job was to get them to lease office space in the properties he represented. But he rarely prepared for a call, didn't make discreet inquiries of employees to get a reading on their present satisfactions or possible future needs. Willie didn't show how his properties could possibly solve a problem. He didn't go in with a list of companies that use his properties. Good testimonial anecdotes were not part of his presentation. He simply gave out brochures, told prospects what properties he had, and the square foot price. Willie left Houston for Denver, but he didn't realize office leasing was competitive everywhere.

POOR RECORDS

Bonnie Bigwheel couldn't be bothered with close record keeping of the calls she made or letters she sent. She didn't put down key bits of information that were mentioned in the interviews, such as names of prospect's children and prospect's interests. She didn't even track usual buying quantities or the prospect's buying pattern. Her prospect records weren't up to date. Phone numbers, notes, vital information, ended up on any scrap of paper, misplaced, never transferred to one notebook or file system. Bonnie felt above details. In fact, she was a little proud of the fact that her record keeping was lousy, that she was a right-brain type of gal who thought in concepts, not little facts. That's for left-brain bean counters.

NEGATIVE ATTITUDE

Gary Gloomdoom sells computer software. If you're around him for five minutes you know everything is awful. His customers are stupid, or a pain in the neck, and expect too darn much. His company is unfair in the way accounts are assigned, or the bonus system isn't right, or the policies are idiotic. Management doesn't know what it's doing. They ought to cut the price—the competition is killing him. He's got the worst territory, and nobody appreciates that fact. He heard rumors that the company might cut back; that things look bad for the industry; that it could get worse next year.

Gloomdoom will really hang a cloud on you. Go to lunch with him and you're depressed for the rest of the day.

OFFICE CLINGER

Curley Clinger is like a bee that won't leave the hive to get honey. There's always some trivia on the desk that needs attention. So he'll make sales calls tomorrow. But tomorrow there's more desk trivia that needs to be taken care of. No use making sales calls before 10:00 A.M. People are opening their mail. But 10:00 A.M. is coffee break. Curley lets everybody know when it's coffee time. After coffee there are some people in the office he needs to check with. Then, of course, at 11:30 A.M. everybody will be getting ready to go to lunch. So that's no time to make calls. And no use calling on them before 1:30 or 2:00 P.M., since they won't be back yet. And 4:00 P.M. is certainly a bad time to make calls since people are getting ready to go home.

Friday afternoons aren't good at all. Prospects are getting ready for the weekend. Clinger even has an excuse for not making calls if it's raining or if it's bright and sunny.

POOR LISTENING HABITS

Gilroy Gliblips was trying to sell a health maintenance plan to a large plant in St. Louis. He was talking to the personnel director, but he wouldn't listen. In fact, once he started talking he wouldn't even come up for air. He went on and on about the benefits of his plan. Finally, the personnel director grabbed him.

"Hold it, will you! I no longer work here. The company's just been sold to another corporation." Gliblips never heard about the six-month study that showed that the top 10 percent of salespeople do one-third the talking that the bottom 10 percent do.

PERSONAL MATTERS FIRST

Chad Charming has lots of enthusiasm. Trouble is, most of it is spent on his personal interests. He'd hang on the phone with some gal he was dating. You'd hear sudden bursts of laughter. Half the messages in his box were personal calls. Then there was that outboard motor he was buying. For a week he spent half of each day shopping around. At his desk he'd be looking over the various brochures, sometimes interrupting others with comments. Chad always had some personal errand to do; a bill to pay or a run to the bank or out to get a hair cut. He really enjoyed lunches. They'd run an hour and a half to two hours. Chad usually came in a little late and left a little early. Three forty-five to 4:00 P.M. was wrap up time . . . time to go meet a friend for happy hour at Zanies.

POOR APPEARANCE AND MANNERS

Cooty Uncouth wiped his mouth with the back of his hand, then yelled over his shoulder, "Hey waiter, gimmie the check."

Cooty chewed with his mouth open and stabbed at food with his fork. He always ate with his fork pointed down. He talked with his mouth full, hunched over his food as he shoveled it in. Trouble was, Cooty wasn't having lunch in a foundry. He was trying to sell mutual funds to a prospect who didn't appreciate his manners.

Cooty usually picked his teeth when he got back to the office. Maybe he needed to. He had a black cavity in one of the bicuspids. Cooty's shoes needed a shine. If he wore anything dark, there were sprinkles of dandruff on it. A spot on the tie didn't matter; neither did those grubby fingernails. He really needed to carry some mints. Cooty never understood why people backed away when he talked. One thing: Cooty was consistent. His appearance, his car, his brief-case, his desk were all the same—a mess.

TIGHT CIRCLE OF CALLS

Digger Deeprut makes the same old pattern of calls. It's not that he's afraid to make new calls. It's just that he's made good friends with all his customers. And he services them well. In fact, he overservices. Of course they love him. But he doesn't make time for new calls. He's in a service rut. Digger doesn't know that he has to make new calls just to stay even, that the average attrition of lost customers runs 15 to 25 percent annually, depending on the industry. If he used the phone less for those "touch base" calls, he could release needed time for new calls.

EXAGGERATING

Sidney Slicktongue tells them what they want to hear. He's quick with answers. It doesn't matter if they're not always correct. Sid just cannot make a presentation without exaggerating. It's a habit. He lays it on thick and bluffs through any question. Sid can unload half truths without wavering an eye. He almost believes his own stories.

Fortunately, the slick tongues are on the way out in selling. Buying and selling has changed. Today's informed, sophisticated buyer just doesn't have time for them anymore.

There they are, thirteen of them. If you've got just one hanging on your back, toss that devil now. It may be costing you more than you realize.

18

Mapping Your Strategy

A study was made of alumni ten years out of Harvard to find out how many were achieving their goals. An astounding 83 percent had no goals at all! Fourteen percent had specific goals, but they weren't written down. Their average earnings were three times what those in the 83 percent group were earning. However, the three percent who had written goals were earning ten times that of the 83 percent group!

Further studies with other groups found the above figures to be quite consistent. Most people do not have goals, much less written ones. In fact, this constant talk about goals is annoying to many. I can say that I have been one of those who has been bored by so much motivational talk about "goals." Therefore, in this chapter I'm going to change the word to "objectives." Somehow, that sounds better.

Without planned objectives we simply comply with any emotional feeling of the moment, including influence and pressure from others. Add to that a combination of habit patterns from the past. Various wishful thoughts about what to do with our lives chase through our minds, but without planned objectives there is no commitment. Without commitment there are no new patterns taking place in the brain's neurons. Without this Mind Set there is no intense flow of intuitive messages from inside and from without.

These are the messages that tell us how to accomplish our objectives. When there is a purpose our brain seems to be a constant sounding board of ways to get over and around obstacles. One idea spawns another. What seems like luck to some observers is not luck at all. We are drawn to ideas, events, and people of like nature. Opportunities open. Thought vibrations of our commitments find their targets.

LONG-RANGE COMMITMENT

As soon as possible, take a drive alone to someplace that is serene; somewhere without people distractions, but where you will feel safe. Try to do it when there is no time pressure on you. You want to feel free to just sit there, whether it's an hour or two. Sit very still, then ask yourself, "What gives meaning to my life?"

That is a powerful question to ask yourself. Wait for some answers to bubble forth. One may not come immediately. Don't get impatient. Don't be overly concerned about it. You may have to make another trip to the spot. You may have to make several.

What you're after are those deep feelings of what really counts to you. Millions of people are chasing other peoples' objectives. Many of these are societies' objectives. Going after objectives that aren't really felt, but are "the thing to do," or "the thing expected," leads one to endless days of dissatisfactions and uneasiness about life. Relief from this constant undercurrent is sought in the frantic pursuit of fun and diversion. If you intensely want a large income, it must be *your* objective. Otherwise, you will find both the pursuit and the accomplishment empty. I know a thirty-six-year-old doctor who is bored with his profession. Being a doctor was his parent's objective. He would really like to own and operate a marina.

This doesn't mean we can or should shirk our responsibilities. If we have a family it is our responsibility to provide for them. We may have to do some things on a short-term basis. For example, a couple in their late thirties are planning and making arrangements to live on a small island in the Caribbean. Their children are still in school in Atlanta, and they'll make the move as soon as the children are out of high school. In the meantime he is selling medical equipment to hospitals and loves it. She is doing something she really enjoys, teaching art.

As you quietly sit there in your car, do not be too judgmental of ideas. Don't be too concerned at this point with what others might think. Rather, concern your evaluation with trade-offs. What would you have to give up? What hours of training would it take? If you're interested in top management, what are the sacrifices involved?

What is your real motive for wanting to move, or do a certain thing? In doing so, what will you trade, and what will you gain?

Your long-range plans can shift. Nothing wrong with that. New evaluations may change your desires. Simply formulate a new plan. The idea is always to have some kind of direction that is meaningful to *you*. You'll feel better about yourself. Planned direction enhances self-confidence. Your self-esteem is reflected in the way you walk, talk, and express yourself. Your planned direction will focus your energies. It is like the sun's rays coming through a magnifying glass. Focus the energies to one spot and the paper burns. Constantly move the magnifying glass and nothing happens.

Your long-range plan should mesh with your daily living. Almost all your decisions regarding earnings, what you buy, your present work, what you do with free time, and people you cultivate, should be in harmony with your deeply felt direction.

THREE-YEAR PLAN

Following the long-range plan, write your objectives for the next three years. These should include income, any plans regarding location change, family plans, hobby plans, fitness plans, social plans, and business plans. The long-range plan can be general in scope, allowing for changes. This one, however, should be quite specific. And it should closely tie in with your long-range desires. If they don't fit together, then perhaps you're kidding yourself on the long-range plan. It may need rewriting. Your values or desires may have changed.

NINETY-DAY STRATEGY

Now we're into the real guts of Mapping Your Strategy. Aside from mind programming, this is top priority in achieving what you want. Ninety-day planning has teeth in it. It's in the here and now. It feels very real. Your ninety-day strategy will greatly influence all your achievements. The reason is that long-range planning and three-year planning do not seem quite real. It's like being twenty-five years old and knowing that one day you will be fifty-five. You logically know it's real, but it doesn't feel real, so you don't take it too seriously.

Even one year can seem too far away. Critical activity is apt to be put off. But ninety days is very real, and you're more likely to track your progress daily in that period of time.

Get those items down on paper where they'll be seen every day. Put down the specific things you plan to accomplish in the next ninety days. Under each one, put down exactly how you will do it. Think this through. Make it detailed.

Lee Iacocca, in his excellent autobiography, uses the ninety-day plan very effectively with the people reporting to him. He gets *them* to set the ninety-day objectives. They must furnish him with a *written plan* of how they will accomplish each objective. At the end of ninety days they meet again and if they did not achieve some part of the plan they explain why. He is not judgmental; he simply listens. And then new ninety-day objectives are submitted. This master salesman knows how to move his people to maximum self-motivation. The ninety-day plan is one of the keys.

You can do the same yourself. You are reporting to yourself, so to speak, on each item, objectively going over why any item wasn't accomplished. Following that, write out a new ninety-day plan, including the written "how it will be accomplished" part.

Suggestion: Right now, put on your calendar "ninety-day evaluation" at each three-month segment from the date you plan to start. This will be a reminder to keep the ninety-day strategy on track.

These are some suggested ideas for a ninety-day plan:

1. Selling: What are the specific accounts you plan to go after? Exactly how do you plan to go after each one?
2. Presentation: How can you make your presentation more effective? What new visuals and testimonial anecdotes should you inject?
3. Time management: What will you cut out in order to free up time to accomplish what you want? Write in the estimated hours for this.
4. Interest or hobby: Do something you've been putting off.
5. Social: Cultivate some new friends.
6. Family: Schedule new planned activity.
7. Appearance: Prepare a fitness program or specific changes in clothes, hair, and the like.
8. Charisma influence: New habit you want to form such as attentive listening.

It is important that you don't become disheartened or feel guilty when, after ninety days, you have only done part of your program. Simply look at it objectively and try to determine why. Lost interest? Got lazy? Okay, you're not alone. Possibly you put down too much. Perhaps you wrote it all down then never looked at it. That has been my own biggest problem: not glancing at it each and every day.

Immediately formulate the new plan. It may include some of the things that you didn't accomplish in the previous ninety days. Be sure you make everything so specific that you can check off the things that have been done. Make it a game with yourself. See how much you can check off.

Daily "To-Do" List

This must tie right in with your ninety-day plan. Keep it simple. Keep it realistic timewise:

1. Try to write it out the evening before or very early in the morning. Definitely avoid planning your day at nine in the morning.
2. Evaluate the priority of each item with a quick *A*, *B*, or *C* next to it.
3. Go after the *A* items first.
4. Expect daily adjustments according to changing conditions.
5. Refer to the list throughout the day.

COMPETITIVE STRATEGY

If you were a commander on the battlefield, you would put yourself in the enemy's shoes. You would ask yourself, "How do they think? Where are they overconfident? What are their strengths? Where are their weaknesses?" Think this way about your three closest competitors. Try to get a "feel" from their side of the fence. If possible, get some input on the actual representative who calls on the accounts you want.

To outflank competition, do these four things:

1. Formulate a campaign, including a long-range call pattern interspersed with phone calls, regular mailings, and any possible personal cultivation.

2. An assumptive attitude should permeate all your contacts. This does not mean being overly aggressive or cocky. It is the quiet warmth of expectancy. You fully expect to handle the account *regardless* of present circumstances.
3. Get detailed information on the company. Decide ways in which you can help this company, the influencers, and the final decision-maker. Keep in mind that your sincere interest in these people can, in itself, be a strong help.
4. Do those things the competition isn't doing or doesn't want to do.

CALL PATTERN STRATEGY

Go where the money is! Go for the greatest potential. You cannot see everyone. At best, you only have three or four hours out of the day face-to-face with prospects. Get the most out of those hours. Look at the following nationwide figures, the breakdown of gross sales income to corporations:

> Sixty-five percent of the dollars come from 15 percent of the customers. (An *A* account)
> Twenty percent of the dollars come from 20 percent of the customers. (A *B* account)
> Fifteen percent of the dollars come from 65 percent of the customers. (A *C* account)

Go after the *A* potential accounts. You cannot be exceptional in selling if much of your prospecting is on *C* prospects. That doesn't mean ignoring prospects that may order very little. You must measure the category by the *potential*. If the potential isn't there, drop it, let your competitors tie up their time on it, or handle it by phone. Potential should be related to net profit. It may not always be wise to pursue only the largest corporations. You might get into some severe price-cutting with the competition. You must bracket that segment of the market that offers you and your company the greatest potential for profit, and go after the *A* accounts in that bracket.

Go where the power is! Prior to making personal contact with a prospective account, find out who has the influence. Get on the telephone and call people at that company who would be unlikely to make the final decision. Ask them for their help. Tell them you're planning to make a presentation there but that you would like to know who would make the *final* decision on buying what you sell. Then, assuming you have a good phone rapport with them, ask who else might influence the buying decision.

There are two statistics* that are elsewhere in this book and are so important they need to be repeated:

1. Sixty-four percent of all sales calls are made on the wrong person.
2. Eighty percent of sales are made after the fifth callback, yet 80 percent of salespeople quit after the second or third callback.

Form a realistic callback strategy. This may include a certain number of systematic mail, phone, and personal calls. Let your intuition, coupled with economic reality, give you a plan on this. Test the pattern. Fine tune it for best results. Then *stick* with the plan . . . with *every* prospect.

Push your "rejection barrier." A great many salespeople have a hard time with rejection. That may come as a surprise to many people, who think anyone in sales has a thick skin. Actually, salespeople have a great deal of empathy. They must have this sensitivity to be successful. This very sensitivity, plus high ego, can make rejection hard to handle. The problem is that they confuse a turndown of the product or service with personal rejection. It is not the same.

They will, consciously or unconsciously, do almost anything to avoid what they feel is personal rejection. Therefore, they quit making those follow-up calls far too soon. This single fact gives you quite an edge in outflanking competition and bringing in the high-potential accounts. Treat it like a game. Constantly strive to push your "rejection barrier" farther and farther.

Get personal. Decide to go deeper than superficial, friendly exchanges. Look over your customer and prospect lists. Think of the decision-makers and the influencers involved. You help solve their problems and needs with your product or service. You care about them personally. Or should. Be concerned with their lives. Jot down on your prospect and customer sheets such items as

---

* Data compiled from studies conducted in 1981–1982 by Patton Communications Inc., Houston. Earlier studies by *Sales Marketing and Management* revealed the same figures.

children's names and ages, birthdays, and any hobbies or special interests. Be alert daily to any article that pertains to a prospect's interest. Tear it out and send it. Be different; go out of your way for people. Oh, how you'll be remembered. Keep in touch by phone. Send short notes. "Out of contact, out of mind" really begins to apply after three or four weeks.

Sell more where you are. Your present customers are also your best prospects. You have an inside track. Which ones could buy more? Which ones have other divisions that might be able to use your product or service? Are you selling your full line to certain customers . . . or possibly assuming they wouldn't be interested?

One last word about your plans: Keep them simple and specific. Clear Mind Set patterns get clear results.

19

Begin

*T*his is a "hands-on" book of how best to persuade and influence others. It is also how to sell yourself on yourself, how to change your habits and maximize your potentials.

But there is a tough problem with this. It is inertia. Think of how many wonderful books and articles you have read that made you want to change something in your life. The best of intentions were there, but nothing happened. Inertia is a very real force of influence in our lives. It holds us in a situation like the heavy pull of gravity. It keeps us from making very necessary changes. It keeps us locked into dull routines. It blocks us from expanding our lives.

Every marketing executive is aware of the growth and decline curve of a product's life. The same can happen in a person's life: we are either growing or declining. For example, in the first years of one's work, there is expectancy and excitement. Then, as we conquer challenges and become more efficient, the routine of sameness sets in. The curve of growth has changed to decline. Feelings of discontent and boredom gnaw at us. We do the same things with the same people in the same places in the same way, day after day. We feel we're in a rut. Apathy keeps us there. We may settle for a nightly habit of hours in front of the TV or several hours each evening in a bar. These are the symptoms of decline.

To keep that curve of growth pointing upward, we must recharge ourselves with new challenges, interests, and people. At work, it could be boldly asking for a new territory or position, or going after an entire new set of challenging accounts. It means finding ways to inject more fun into what we do.

We need change, physical activity, healthy pleasure, stimulation, and recognition. But we must *seek* them. They don't seek us. We must cast out those fears that we can't do something and go after the things we want! A great way to do this is to write and tape a one-minute "commercial" about yourself and listen to it every day.

HOW TO USE THE ONE-MINUTE TAPED PROFILE OF GROWTH

You probably spend hours in your car: what a time to do some mind programming. Not Deep Alpha; you wouldn't want to do that while driving. But, in addition to your regular Deep Alpha programming, listen to your affirmations on tape. Whereas the Deep Alpha programming would concentrate on a few major goals, your one-minute "commercial" would contain many affirmations in the various areas of your life. It puts action into the changes you want. Simply put on tape all those changes you strongly desire. Play it back several times a day as you're driving. Strong neuron patterns of growth will be formed.

To give you an example of a Growth Profile tape, here is one by a forty-two-year old female executive:

"I am finding excellent ways to increase our total sales. I listen well and get good help from others at the office. Today, I have a great sense of humor. It gets better and better every day. I look vibrant. I am losing twelve pounds. I always leave part of the food on my plate. My posture is excellent. My shoulders are back and my stomach in as I walk around and talk with others. I am drawn to new, stimulating people. I walk two miles every day. I feel active and alive. Jeff and I get along great. All problems are melting away. We have warm feelings. Ways are opening up to buy the condo on the water. Love and caring are pouring out to all people in my life. I accept this. It is now programmed."

Positive things changed dramatically for her. By using the spaced repetition of playing the tape a number of times each day, the growth patterns took place. The Growth Profile takes a person off dead-center inertia and changes good intentions to action.

The car is the perfect place to listen since you're probably alone. There won't be anyone to accuse you of being rather strange or on some kind of ego trip. Play it for thirty days and retape it for the next month, making any changes you desire.

See how it gets rid of fears and moves you into stimulating action and experiences. The entire magic is in the neuron changes of your brain. Your life is changing because your programmed attitude has changed.

Famed psychologist William James said, "The greatest discovery of my generation is that people can actually alter their lives by merely altering their attitudes of mind."

You will alter your Mind Set to those deep-felt wants. As you put this book down, I leave you with just one word . . . *begin*.